Marlborough Revisited
and
The War Remembered

A G.I. Bride Looks Back

MARGARET H. WHARTON

Margaret H Wharton

'Tis, but I cannot name it, 'tis the sense
  Of majesty, and beauty and repose,
A blended holiness of earth and sky,
  Something that makes this individual spot,
This small abiding place of many men,
  A termination and a last retreat.
A centre . . . a whole . . .

William Wordsworth

ALAN SUTTON
1987

Alan Sutton Publishing
Brunswick Road · Gloucester

First published 1987

British Library Cataloguing in Publication Data

Wharton, Margaret H.
    Marlborough revisited and the war
    remembered.
    1. Marlborough (Wiltshire)—Social life
    and customs
    I. Title
    942.3'17   DA690.M46

    ISBN 0-86299-318-0

Jacket photograph: *Mr. and Mrs David Wharton; married
15 March 1944*

Typesetting and origination by
Alan Sutton Publishing Limited
Photoset Bembo 11/12
Printed in Great Britain

This book is dedicated to the memory of

Jess E. Chandler 1911–1985

ACKNOWLEDGEMENTS

I am indebted to the following Marlborough residents who have given me help and encouragement in my writing endeavours:– Mr Robert Ashley, Mrs Rose Chandler, Mrs Eric Free, Mr & Mrs Oscar Fulk, Mr Philip Garside, Mr James Glover, Mrs Muriel Gough, Mrs R. Kerrison, Mr Nigel Kerton, Dr & Mrs Dick Maurice.

I also wish to thank my many American friends for their interest, and I wish to make special mention of the following:– Mrs Emily Aumiller of Upper Saddle River, New Jersey, English teacher at Ramsey (N.J.) High School, Dr James R. Caldwell, retired History professor from the University of North Carolina, Dr Jane Gabin, proprietor of Westminster Alley British Shop in Chapel Hill and Mrs Jean Hunter, longtime English friend from Houston and El Paso, Texas.

I owe thanks, too, to my two sons – to David, a doctoral candidate at the University of Texas for a paper he wrote on the development of the American small town as shown in history and literature, which gave me a new perspective on the English town of Marlborough, and to Christopher, a graduate student in journalism at the University of North Carolina who gave me editorial assistance, particularly in the arrangement of the text.

Lastly I am most grateful to my husband David, for assuming the practical tasks of copying, mailing and making travel arrangements, as well as for his ever present patience and understanding.

MARGARET H. WHARTON

CONTENTS

BIBLIOGRAPHY

ADAMS, W. MAURICE: Savernake Forest, Wolfhall, Tottenham House and the Battle of Bedwyn.

BRADLEY, A. G.: Round About Wiltshire, 1943.

BRENTNALL, H. C. and CARTER, C. C.: The Marlborough Country, 1932.

BRIGGS, SUSAN: The Home Front, 1975.

CARDIGAN, The Earl of: The Wardens of Savernake Forest, 1949.

CHANDLER, J. E.: A History of Marlborough, 1977.

DOWDING, M. K.: Old Wiltshire Market Towns and Villages 1896.

DRABBLE, MARGARET: A Writer's Britain, 1979.

DRYDEN, ALICE: Memorials of Old Wiltshire, 1906.

FEDDEN, ROBIN and JOEKES, ROSEMARY: The National Trust Guide to England, 1974.

FELLOWS, ARNOLD: The Wayfarers' Companion 1937.

HAWKES, JACQUETTA: Early Britain 1945.

LEE, HELENE R.: Bittersweet Decision, 1986.

LEETE-HODGE, LORNIE: Moonraker County, 1982.

Lucy's Marlborough Directory, 1931

STEDMAN, A. R.: Marlborough and the Upper Kennet Country, 1960. A History of Marlborough Grammar School, 1944.

TREVELYAN, G. M.: History of England, 1926.

I

INTRODUCTION

"Oh, to be in England,
Now that April's there."
Robert Browning

And after 39 years I was indeed in England in April! I had returned
many times, but in June, August, September, October and even
May, but never before April. And in 1985 April's weather was very
disappointing – not even an April shower followed by quick clearing
and a watery sun appearing to make the raindrops sparkle with all the
colours of the rainbow – just a persistent bone-chilling wind out of
grey lowering skies. Nevertheless a promised hint of spring was in
the air, and the promise was fulfilled in the rare moments when the
sun chased away the grey, and puffy white clouds scudded across the
sky, briefly but brilliantly blue. The wild plum, known as the
blackthorn was in full bloom, its white blossom coating the black
stems so that the hedgerows appeared snow-sprinkled – it was
almost cold enough. I had heard old country folk, my mother among
them, talk of the blackthorn winter, a cold spell that seemed to come
when the blossom is out in early spring. In 1985 I experienced it as
never before. But the cold winds seemed no deterrent to the flowers,
wild or cultivated. Hosts of daffodils were waving and dancing in the
breeze, tulips of all hues were in full bloom, their flowers so large we
wondered how the stems could support them, while rock plants,
purple, yellow and white cascaded over grey stone walls in cottage
gardens. In the woods shy primroses, modest blue violets and fragile

1

pink-veined anemones appeared to welcome spring. The birds, too, the thrush, chaffinch, robin and blackbird sang joyously and, preening their mating plumage, went busily about the all-consuming task of nest building. And what a thrill it was to hear once more the cuckoo heralding a new day with his unmistakable call! And then after April, when May followed, the fruit trees burst into bloom and became so heavily laden with blossom that nothing of the trees could be seen but trunks supporting the white of pear and plum, the pale pink of apple and the rosier hue of ornamental cherry. In the woods bluebells spread their misty blue carpets and in the farmlands flowering rape fields added solid shapes of acid yellow to the patchwork browns of ploughed and fallow fields, the fresh green of grass and sprouting grain. Great trees, still bare for the most part, were timidly showing just a hint of green, and white, pink-tipped daisies, yellow buttercups and dandelions dotted the fields, where young calves frisked and lambs gambolled beside their woolly mothers, fortuitously as yet unshorn.

Apart from enjoying springtime, it proved a good time for me to be in England and Marlborough. The war which ended forty years ago was very much on people's minds. War reminiscences, reunions, visits to former battlegrounds and war stations, bookshops featuring war stories, all combined to create the right climate for my small chronicle of one Englishwoman's wartime experiences and subsequent life in America, preceded as they were by an account of childhood and schooldays in Marlborough that told not just my story but that of many of my contemporaries.

This time we were the guests of Oscar and Joan Fulk, staying in the house they own in Herd Street. It is one of Marlborough's older homes, tastefully modernized and comfortably furnished with appropriate antiques, and staying there we enjoyed a warm hospitality which the impersonal atmosphere of a hotel could not have given us. Joan and Oscar have been friends for many years. Theirs is the G.I. bride story in reverse, Joan the English bride and Oscar the American groom who chose to make their home in England rather than in the States. We have much in common, Joan a Marlborough girl and Grammar School old student as I was, Oscar a North Carolinian and wartime soldier like my husband, our experiences, paradoxically, parallel yet widely divergent.

Because every country town however small answers the needs – commercial, governmental, educational and cultural of the district surrounding it, the character of each such town is determined by and reflects the locality it serves. Marlborough is no exception. The downs, Savernake Forest, the Kennet, the villages of chalkland and woodland, of river valley and Pewsey Vale, have all played their part in the town's development and each has helped to mould the face of Marlborough as we observe it today. Therefore we will consider each area in turn in an endeavour to study the town and its changing face. I will begin with the chalk downs, for they have provided the predominant influence, and will proceed thence to Savernake Forest, the River Kennet and the surrounding villages, eventually arriving at the very hub of the area, Marlborough itself.

II

THE PLACE

Chapter 1

THE DOWNS

> "... all my soul was dancing ...
> Dancing with a measured step
> from wrecked and shattered towns
> Away ... upon the Downs."
> Edward Wyndham Tennant

There is a wide belt of chalk running through England from the south coast to Flamborough Head in the east beginning and ending in the chalk cliffs that mark our coasts. In the center another great spur goes off to the south east to become the South Downs which end in the white cliffs of Dover, cliffs that symbolize home and England to so many seafaring wanderers. These belts of chalk come together in Wiltshire and the Marlborough Downs are among their highest and wildest parts. The steep escarpment that marks the western edge of the chalk divides Wiltshire into two very different areas, "chalk", and "cheese". The "cheese" to the west of the escarpment is a rich lowland of dairy and arable farmland while to the east is the "chalk", the high exposed tableland known as the Marlborough Downs. The town, Marlborough, is situated in the midst of this downland, but in a hollow on the banks of the Kennet, the only river of any size to cut through this high plateau. Because the middle and upper chalk is hard and porous, it has resisted denudation and forms the rolling uplands of the downs. The Marlborough Downs extend from the Pewsey Vale in the south, to

5

the Swindon Plain in the north, and the west to Devizes and Salisbury Plain. In the east they merge with the Berkshire Downs.

The Marlborough Downs have all the characteristics of chalk land – wide vistas, vast unfenced stretches of short springy turf, white roads looping like ribbons over green hillsides patched with chalk outcroppings, clumps and avenues of great beeches, planted to give some protection from the winds that sweep across the open downs, water meadows, clear streams lined with willows and elms and bordered with villages of thatch and stone and flint clustered around their ancient churches. It is a land of rolling hills, steep escarpments, dry valleys, White Horses, prehistoric earthworks, camps, burial mounds and mysterious temples. Roman roads cut through the downs with here and there the remains of camps and villas, while today the downs support innumerable sheep and many racing stables and are the training grounds for soldiers and airmen of the twentieth century.

Agriculturally the Marlborough Downs have always been considered of low value. This is largely due to lack of water. The chalk is covered with a thin layer of topsoil, thicker in the hollows, thinning on the slopes and almost non-existent on the hilltops where the white chalk often shows through the thin grass. The downs, in the past, were considered good only for sheep, which animals roamed the downs by day, saving what soil there was by their constant treading and enriching it with their droppings, so that a fine sweet grass was produced which nourished them and made their meat tender and their wool fine. At night the sheep were brought down from the hillsides and put out in folds in the valleys by their shepherds, folds which were fenced by hurdles beautifully woven from pliant wood. Hurdle making is a rural craft which is fast dying out.

Before the Industrial Revolution the wool from the downland farms found its way to the cloth industries of West Country towns such as Bath, Corsham, Bradford-on-Avon, Castle Combe in Wiltshire and Cirencester in Gloucestershire. Flemish weavers were brought in to teach their skills to the local workers, who produced fine cloth in a cottage type industry. Some of these towns grew very rich and some built fine buildings in gratitude and thanks for their prosperity. The huge church at Cirencester is a fine example of a 'wool' church. Marlborough was never a 'wool' town in the way these western towns were, but she was, and still is, the site of the great sheep fairs generally held twice a year sometimes in the High Street, but on the Common in more recent times. But when machines began to replace men the wool industry moved away from Wiltshire and the west, north to Yorkshire, where there was an abundance of coal and iron for power and machinery, good water from the Pennine streams, while the raw wool came from the sheep of the Yorkshire moors. The downland farmers with a less ready market for their wool had no option but to reduce the number of their sheep and look for alternative means of farming for survival.

In the early days of sheep farming, the water shortage was partly overcome by the construction of dewponds. Three are now left in the Marlborough area, Totterdown, Sugar Pond on Martinsell and Oxenmere on Tan Hill, thought to be the oldest since it is mentioned in a Saxon document of 905 A.D. Layers of straw, chalk and clay lined a depression which was then 'started' with a small amount of water, which the ancients believed attracted more water. Though called dewponds the moisture comes rather from rain, mist and fog and most continued to function even when there was a prolonged period of dry weather. The art of making them is now lost and there is still some uncertainty about how or why they worked. Better methods of irrigation and deeper wells which tap the sources of water known to exist underground have enabled some of the downland to be put down to arable cultivation – this was especially encouraged during the war – and more dairy farming is now carried on. With the decrease in the numbers of sheep, there is less of the springy turf formerly so typical of the downland and more coarse grass, gorse and scrub grows in its place. Sheep however do seem to be returning in greater number to the downs of Wiltshire – at least I gain that impression as I make my periodic visits. I am glad to see them. Sheep and downland to my mind go together.

It is on the high downland that we find the first signs of man's settlement. Here in the wide open spaces he could roam and build his first primitive habitations, find flint for his weapons, sarsen stones for his temples, find a measure of safety from wild animals, while the lowlands and river valleys remained an impassable morass of swamp and bog. The only evidence in the town itself of any habitation by prehistoric peoples is the mound in the College grounds, though why, when and by whom it was thrown up we do not know and can only conjecture.

The chalk uplands form a rolling country of round backed ridges separated by deep wide valleys. Though he is thinking of the South Downs, Kipling calls them "our blunt, bow-headed, whale-backed Downs" and his description fits the Marlborough Downs well enough. The uplands form open grassy downs, dotted with stunted thorn and scrub, scored with tracks left by rain and with patches of white chalk showing through. Sheep graze the short springy turf and keep it fertilized and the land is ideal for gallops and the training of racehorses which for many years now has been important economically to this part of Wiltshire and has brought romance, colour and new people into the area. The topsoil is very thin but where clay with flints appear then the downland can be cultivated and woodlands such as Savernake Forest appear. The action of water on the chalk has cut valleys which have been deepened and widened through the ages. Many of these valleys are dry for at least part of the year but there is underground water which has shaped the land by erosion and percolation. In the upper chalk many bands of flint appear. Flints are nodules of silica that have collected round marine animal remains such as sea urchins and sponges. They are very hard and dense, but can be split, chipped and shaped relatively easily. The men of the Stone Age by a process of accident, trial and error, learned early to shape flints into arrow and axe and spear heads and many of these primitive weapons have beeen found on the downs. Also in the downland areas, though in the valleys rather than on the heights, are found Sarsen stones, huge blocks of gritty sandstone believed to be survivals of the sands which once covered North Wiltshire. They are sometimes called Druid stones, because they formed the raw material of temples such as Avebury and Stonehenge, and sometimes Grey Wethers, because of their resemblance from a distance to a flock of sheep, "wether" being an old word for a sheep. They are far fewer now than formerly because from prehistoric times on they have been broken up by alternate applications of fire and water and used for building material. Many were broken up as recently as 1880 to build the railway bridges between Marlborough and Andover. Flints too are used extensively in local building, often being arranged in patterns alternating with stone for walls, cottages and barns. They were used at one time for roads, but their hard points caused many punctures and a great deal of dust in dry weather, so the practice has been discontinued. White horses have become a symbol of the chalk country. On certain hillsides the turf has been removed to expose the white chalk underneath in the figure of a horse and there are four in the immediate area of Marlborough, one in the town itself on Granham Hill, the others at Pewsey, Alton and Cherhill. None are very old, the oldest, largest and most lifelike being the one at Cherhill which was cut in 1780. The oldest and least life like of these horses is the one at Uffington which is not in Wiltshire at all, but in Berkshire, and it has given its name to a broad fertile valley, the Vale of the White Horse. The White Horse at Westbury is the oldest in Wiltshire and it was first cut to mark the site of King Alfred's victory over the Danes at Edington over a thousand years ago. Its appearance was changed in 1778 to make it more horselike and most people will agree that it is a very handsome beast and can be seen to advantage on the steep hillside. Other chalk figures appear elsewhere on the downs. The New Zealanders cut a huge figure of a kiwi at Tidworth in World War I and at a village called Fovant on Salisbury Plain soldiers stationed there cut their regimental badges, while the Australians left a map of their land and a huge kangaroo stark white against the green turf.

Hilaire Belloc once wrote that "chalk should somewhere be warmly hymned and praised by every man who belongs to the south of England for it is the meaning of good land". Three fifths of Wiltshire is chalk and it is chalk which has endowed the county with its characteristic appearance, its history, its way of life and made it the good land that it is to all its sons and daughters. Chalk gives it its bare rolling hills, gives it the turf that brings the sheep. Thorn and juniper are among the few indigenous trees, though the beech planted in clumps and avenues to provide windbreaks likes the chalk so well that many people think it a native tree. These graceful trees add much to the beauty of the downland.

The downs are often represented in literature as bleak, empty, monotonous, terrifying, prone to driving rain and bitter winds, but for the native and discerning visitor they represent a rare kind of beauty. The Reverend Gilpin, a prolific describer of rural landscape in the 18th century did not like the downs – "the chalk," he says, "spoils everything", and he thought the Marlborough Downs "a vast dreary scene". But some writers have praised the downs, delighting in the clean uncluttered line of hills against the ever changing sky and the air of remote mystery they conjure up.

The lines at the beginning of this chapter were written by Edward Wyndham Tennant when he was at Laventie in Northern France during World War I. When spring came to the war shattered town he thought of home and England and the downs and for a moment his heart went dancing. Charles Hamilton Sorley, an old Marlburian and a casualty of that same war, immortalized the town and its downland setting in the poem *Marlborough*. Another poet, Edward Thomas, who also lost his life in Flanders in 1917, although a Londoner by birth, wrote lovingly of the downland country he grew to know when he spent holidays with an aunt and grandmother at Swindon.

His best work perhaps was a moving biography he wrote of his Wiltshire hero, Richard Jefferies. For Richard Jefferies was the prose poet and philosopher of Wiltshire. He was born at Coate near Swindon in a long low farmhouse on the Marlborough road. I have passed it and seen its memorial plaque many times, my father in childhood invariably pointing the house out as the birthplace of Jefferies, long before I had any conception of who he was or why he was famous. For most of his life he was a struggling journalist, prone to wander by himself through the countryside so that he earned the title of "mad Dick Jefferies". He wrote all his life, mostly bad novels which publishers rejected time and time again, but when he wrote "*Bevis*", the autobiographical *The Story of My Heart* and *The Gamekeeper at Home* his true genius became apparent. Liddington Hill, Tan Hill, White Horse Hill, Coate Water, the chalk country of Wiltshire were to him what the Lakes were to Wordsworth, Dorset to Hardy, Bredon Hill to Housman, the Yorkshire Moors to the Brontes, and some critics have compared him to Thoreau.

Like Belloc, William Cobbett, author of *Rural Rides* in the late 18th and early 19th centuries extols the chalk country, and the downland of Salisbury Plain provides the dark tragic background for several of Thomas Hardy's novels. The final scene in *Tess of the d'Urbevilles* is played out at Stonehenge where "the wind whistles mournfully between the monoliths and the sheep crop the grass on the ancient barrows which lie in the shadow of the dead temple". He calls a large barrow "a featureless convexity of chalk and soil" and takes satisfaction in the gloomy aspect of the downs, the often inclement weather, the mysterious stone circles and the lonely gibbets.

Those of us who live or have lived in the Marlborough vicinity are never very far from some strange relic of human history. Stonehenge on Salisbury Plain is only 20 miles from Marlborough and Avebury larger and older though not as spectacular as the better known temple is only 5 miles away. Nearby is the massive mound of Silbury, the Roman road deviating from its straight course to go around it. On the downs everywhere are the barrows or grave mounds of a race long vanished while earthworks, hilltop camps and prehistoric "castles" stand guard against the mysterious enemies of the early peoples. Such antiquities brought many people to Wiltshire. John Aubrey, learned historian born near Kington St. Michael, discovered Avebury accidentally while out hunting with a party from Marlborough. Very impressed with its size and scope he wrote that to compare Stonehenge with Avebury was like comparing a parish church to a cathedral. Later he escorted King

Charles II to the top of Silbury Hill. Samuel Pepys also climbed the great mound and went to Old Sarum by night, which he called "prodigious, so as to fright me to be in it alone at that time of night". Learned people have pieced together a remote past from the flint arrowheads, spears and utensils that have been found on the downs, along with pottery, jewelled ornaments and bones, animal and human. Using the most modern methods of detection and research there is still much that remains a mystery. Many have explored the ancient roads that remain as green tracks across the downs. The Ridgeway, super highway of prehistoric Britain, follows the high curve of the Marlborough Downs and links up with other green roads. The Wansdyke, thought to be a defensive line constructed when the Roman legions were withdrawn in the fifth century goes for miles across the downs. A good view of it can be obtained from the road between Beckhampton and Devizes. Thousands of men must have dug the ditch and thrown up the rampart which seems to stretch into infinity.

Though when living in Marlborough I spent less time on the downs than in Savernake Forest and the fields of the Kennet – after all we lived on the south east of town which made the forest easier of access for our walks and picnics than the downs to the north and west, – it was always a pleasure to walk across the Common to get a foretaste of the downs and once or twice we undertook the rather formidable hike to Four Mile Clump. I always liked to drive to Rockley and beyond to Hackpen Hill – what a magnificent view across the Swindon Plain – to take the straight Roman road to Swindon, or go west along the Kennet valley, past the Kennet Long Barrow, to Overton Hill crowned with its ancient graveyard. At Beckhampton, if one takes the south fork to Devizes one crosses one of the wildest stretches of downland country. Slightly north of Beckhampton lies the village of Avebury site of a huge monolitic temple made from the Sarsen stones brought by sheer manpower from the Valley of the Rocks at Lockeridge several miles away. I spent some time there doing an assignment during my college days at the time when Mr Alexander Keiller was doing his excavations, restoration and reconstruction. At Beckhampton there is an ancient inn, The Waggon and Horses. I once stayed there with Eileen Randall a friend from my days at the Grammar School. Her parents kept the inn at that time and I have since had lunch there several times. Like the Castle Inn at Marlborough it was a hostelry where many travellers chose to spend the night rather than face the lonely perils of the downs with darkness drawing on and weather like as not wet or windy or snowing. At the Beckhampton crossroads stands the big red brick Georgian house belonging in my day to horse trainer Fred Darling, an old man when I was a child, very well known in the racing world and commonly known as 'the Guv'nor'.

During the war the Beckhampton racing stables were to be visited on several occasions by Queen Elizabeth when she was a young princess. In 1942, at sixteen her father took her there for the first time to see two special horses, Big Game and Sun Chariot who were trained by Fred Darling and often ridden to victory by Gordon Richards. The latter had begun his racing career as a local stable lad, but had risen meteorically to champion jockey and was eventually to be knighted by the Queen for his spectacular achievements on the turf. He and his Swindon-born wife and family lived for many years in a beautiful house in the Cardigan Road area of Marlborough. At Beckhampton Princess Elizabeth got her first introduction to many of racing's greats. One of them, Lord Porchester was to become her racing manager, and the Queen and he were to introduce new ideas and innovations into the breeding and training of racehorses. Early on in their association Fred Darling, meticulous and disciplined in his training methods, remarked to Gordon Richards, 'Princess Elizabeth must have a natural eye for a horse'. Her subsequent interest in and achievements in horse racing have more than proved him right.

We once stopped in the shelter of a copse of beeches crowning an eminence on the Chippenham road to watch the Beckhampton lads putting the horses through their paces. What a fine sight to see the strings of thoroughbreds exercising at a gentle trot or sometimes at a full gallop on the short springy turf, though they looked like tiny moving toys in the vast expanse of downland hill and endless sky.

The story goes that a Marlborough boy, his name unknown, went to London like Dick Whittington to seek his fortune. He remained there for fifty years becoming a prosperous merchant but never once returning to the town of his birth. When, an old man, he lay on his deathbed, a friend asked if there was anything he needed. 'Marlborough Downs,' he murmured, 'Marlborough Downs and the rain.'

Chapter 2

THE RIVER KENNET

"For men may come and men may go
But I go on for ever . . ."
Tennyson

First there was the river . . . It is the Kennet that has given the Marlborough country its distinctive topography, carving the chalk into the familiar hills and valleys, and it was the river that brought the first people, for dwelling places are always determined by water supply.

Many aeons ago the chalk extended far to the west, its mass generally tipping towards the east, so that the streams flowed in that direction. The Kennet today is one of the longest remnants of one of these original rivers. Because the Cherwell-Thames was the master stream, smaller streams, the Kennet among them flowed into it, and this pattern has persisted so that the Kennet is one of the main tributaries of the Thames, the confluence being at Reading.

The main source of the Kennet lies in some strong springs at the mouth of Lockeridge Dean, and for some miles it is a half-hearted stream that dries up in summer, but as it flows towards Marlborough it is reinforced by underground streams that increase its volume and it swings along in bold curves, cutting back the outer bank into a steep concave bluff, while the inner bank grows as a long flat tongue of alluvial soil of great fertility. From Manton eastwards this steep bluff can be traced all the way to Reading, beginning at Granham and Postern Hills south of Marlborough. On the opposite side of the valley there is a long gentle slope. The bluff is formed because the river is flowing not along the bottom of the chalk syncline but along its northern slope.

The river flows through a deeply incised valley flanked by water meadows, which are in the flood plain and dependent on irrigation.

This method of irrigation was known to the Romans, but it was in the 17th and 18th centuries that it was further developed and refined. The meadows are traversed by deep trenches and the water is held back by wooden hatches, which are opened and closed by workers known as "drowners", thus alternately flooding and draining the fields. These meadows, the water so regulated, provided spring feed for sheep and lambs in March, April and May, a hay crop in June and cattle pasture in the late summer and fall. They were especially appropriate for the sheep farmer, at one time the main form of agriculture carried on in the chalklands, but are less important in more modern times. Most of the adjoining parishes lie either side of the river, the land of each including water meadows, permanent pasture, arable land and hill pastures which stretch up the sides of the chalk hills out of which the river has carved its valley.

The name "Kennet" belongs to the pre-English period of language, but its meaning has been lost. It has been suggested that the name of the Roman settlement Cunetio was derived from the word "Kennet". When the Saxons came in after the Romans left, they too settled on the Kennet, but they selected the Marlborough area rather than that of Mildenhall where Cunetio was located. It is believed that they hated the Roman settlements and generally chose to build their own huts in virgin territory.

When one walks from the Bath Road to Preshute Church one takes a pedestrian causeway built over the water meadows, across a bridge over the river and so to the little Norman church in its green graveyard full of ancient headstones. It is one of the prettiest little churches to be found anywhere, standing as it does on the banks of the river, with old horse chestnuts throwing their shadows on the clear surface of the water. From there the river goes by way of Treacle Bolly to Marlborough to run parallel to the High Street on its southern side. Lovely gardens run down to its deep and clear chalk waters in a way that reminds me in a simpler fashion of the Backs at Cambridge. And on it goes to the old town mill – how we liked to go "round the mill" when we were children to find my father in his workshop in Angel Yard, being sure to stop on the bridge to look for trout and see the ducks and moorhens. Flowing under the London Road bridge it goes past the garden of my old home, a willow fringed island in its midst almost obscuring the town gas works on the opposite bank.

And thence to Stoney Bridges and to Poulton where it is joined by the Og, past Mildenhall, Axford, Ramsbury, Chilton Foliat passing at Hungerford from Wiltshire into Berkshire. In this stretch of the river can be found some of the best trout fishing in England. One sad note has to struck – the great elms which used to be the glory of this part of the Kennet valley have fallen victim to the dread Dutch elm disease and have either been felled or stand like dead and dying skeletons.

But on goes the river to reach Reading at last where its waters mingle with those of the Thames to end up eventually in the North Sea. And all along its course are strung out villages and little towns such as Marlborough like beads on a shining silver chain.

Chapter 3

THE FOREST

"Majestic Savernake
Raises his wood-crowned brow – prospect sublime."
Anonymous

I do not know where the above quotation came from – I discovered it in an old book about Wiltshire which was among my father's effects. Unfortunately the lines no longer apply for if there is a part of the Marlborough country that has suffered a sad deterioration it is Savernake Forest. I recall very clearly the huge gnarled oaks, the towering beeches, their silver grey trunks glistening in the sunlight, casting a dim green light in the recesses of their shade. I remember too the grassy glades dominated by a single giant tree, the green paths winding through the chest high bracken and the old hawthorn trees gleaming in the spring with their white blossoms and giving off a heady fragrance that seemed the very essence of May. And how thrilled we were to see afar off a herd of fallow deer or catch the even rarer sight of a red stag or doe. The whole forest conveyed an impression of nature's magnificence, controlled and groomed by man's loving care. It is very different now – few really big trees left and shaggy unkempt undergrowth on all sides. Part of it is due simply to the passage of time, helped on by years of benign neglect. An old rhyme about the oak goes thus –

> Three centuries he grows and three centuries he stays
> Supreme in state and in three more decays.

Maybe today we are seeing the death of the forest giants for Savernake is one of our oldest forests, a remnant of the primeval wood that once covered most of our island. Maybe the use to which it had to be put during the war – a place to hide and stockpile ammunition for eventual shipment to the continent – hastened its decay. It is now under the control of the Forestry Commission, leased to them for 999 years by the Ailesbury family and it is to be hoped that with reafforestation and the careful nurture of young trees, Savernake will be restored to its former beauty.

The most famous part of Savernake Forest was an avenue of trees that because of its perfect symmetry came to be known as the Grand Avenue. Today it is a travesty of its former self. The avenue of beech trees extended for about 5 miles from Tottenham House to the Iron Gates that used to stand at the top of the London Road Hill just on the edge of the forest boundary. The straight road going up hill and down dale was lined on either side by magnificent trees whose tall trunks towered upward like the columns of a cathedral, their branches meeting at the top in a perfect arch.
One old writer wrote:

> 'The growth is so regular and so perfect that there is a continuous Gothic arch of green for miles, beneath which one may drive or walk as in the aisles of a forest abbey. Composed principally of beech trees and extending almost 5 miles in length that avenue is, perhaps, the grandest in England if not in the world. Here is the dim religious light in its true perfection; for it is not an avenue composed of a single line of trees on either side, but of trees innumerable spreading far to right and left; their tall, straight trunks rising high in air and their lofty branches thoroughly interlacing overhead, and forming the most complete and perfect pointed arch that eye can see or mind conceive.'

In the middle of the avenue the road widens out into an octagon where the Eight Walks meet. The avenue was planned and planted by the third Earl of Ailesbury in 1723. I am glad he cannot see it today.

On the edge of the forest just off the London Road stands a lovely house called Furze Coppice. In April 1985 the lawns surrounding and approaching it were covered in magnificent daffodils while around the entrance gates stood several giant beech trees, their pointed buds ready to break into leaf if only the sun would shine. It was a corner of the forest looking as I remembered it.

Tottenham House, ancestral home of the Marquess of Ailesbury is situated at the extreme south eastern verge of the forest and is set in what was designed as a deer park bordered by beautiful avenues of beech, dotted with clumps of the same tree and fenced to keep the deer out of the body of the forest. We first hear of a Tottenham

Lodge in the reign of Henry VIII whose love affair with Jane
Seymour brought him to Savernake where he enjoyed good hunting.
Jane lived at a house called Wolfhall near Burbage, a property which
belonged to her family, Seymours who later acquired the titles of
Earl of Hertford and Duke of Somerset. Wolfhall was at that time a
more important house than Tottenham. While historians believe
Henry's marriage to Jane Seymour took place at Hampton Court and
not at Wolfhall as Wiltshire people are prone to say, certain it is that
the marriage feast was held in the great tithe barn, which unfortunately was destroyed by fire in 1960. Of the house at Wolfhall
nothing remains. The present farmhouse is comparatively modern
and the farmyard presents a conglomeration of old farm machinery,
but nearby there is a grove of trees which is still called King Harry's
walk and an old red brick house with tall Tudor chimneys known as
the Laundry. It was in 1582 that Wolfhall was abandoned in favour of
Tottenham as the home of the Somerset family.

The story of Savernake Forest and Tottenham House is of course
the story of the Ailesbury family. Through the many vicissitudes of
history its descent can be traced from the Esturmys of Norman days,
to the Seymours, Hertfords and Somersets of Tudor times, to the
Bruces of the Stuart and Georgian periods and to the Brudenells on
down to the present. The Ailesbury title came to Savernake when
Thomas Bruce, Earl of Ailesbury and Elgin married the Seymour
heiress to the forest in 1678. A descendant became the first marquess
in 1821 being given the higher rank in the birthday honours of
George IV. The Cardigan title was inherited from the Brudenell
branch of the family when the Earl of Cardigan – he who had led the
ill-fated Charge of the Light Brigade at Balaclava in the Crimean
War – died without issue. It was he too who gave his name to the
buttoned woollen jacket he popularized. The Cardigan title became
that of the heir of the marquess, while later the courtesy title of
Viscount Savernake was given to the Earl of Cardigan's oldest son.
The family name is Brudenell-Bruce and that came about in the
following fashion.

In 1747 a young man and fourth son of an Earl of Cardigan
inherited the Ailesbury title from his uncle Charles just before his
18th birthday. His name was Thomas Bruce Brudenell, the latter
being the name of the Cardigans while Bruce came from a long line
of Scottish ancestors on his mother's side. Wishing to identify
himself with his late Uncle's family, who were also of Bruce descent,
he transposed and hyphenated the names Brudenell-Bruce and also
quartered the Bruce coat of arms with his own. In 1761 he married

Susanna, the widowed daughter of wealthy Henry Hoare of Stour-head. They became the direct ancestors of all the Brudenell-Bruces living today.

The name Bruce is one of the oldest in England. A column entitled *Old Families Growing Few* appeared in the *New York Sun* in 1913. Yellowed now with age it was clipped and preserved by my father-in-law because the name Wharton is mentioned in it as another of the oldest names. It has this to say about the Bruces and I quote:

> The Bruce family, now represented by the Earls (sic) of Aylesbury (sic) and Elgin unblushingly stand in the van for the inspection of genealogists. The family is traced back to Thebotaw, a Duke of Norway in the year 721 A.D., from whom was descended that same Rollo who conquered Normandy in 912. A Robert de Brusee occurs in Normandy about the tenth century and one with the same surname emigrated to England about a hundred years later.

This Thomas, Earl of Ailesbury, together with the uncle from whom he inherited was in a large measure responsible for shaping the modern forest. They planted many beeches in avenues and clumps, planted open areas on the edge of the forest with oak, birch and chestnut and cleared rough patches of furze. At this time too with farming methods changing, the farms around Savernake began to assume their present day boundaries. Thomas opened up grassy rides and paths through the woodland, the best known of which are the Grand Avenue and the Eight Walks. Thomas made the land surrounding the house into a vast fenced deer park, with herds of both red and fallow deer. On rising ground, known as Three Oak Hill, at the edge of the deer park and in full view of Tottenham House stands a tall monument known as "The Column". Thomas had purchased it secondhand from Hammersmith, had it brought to Wiltshire in sections and erected it in 1781 as a memorial tribute to the uncle from whom he inherited the Ailesbury earldom. Eight years later another inscription was added which read thus:

> 'In commemoration of a signal instance of Heaven's Providence over these Kingdoms in the year 1789, by restoring to perfect health from a long and afflicting disorder, our excellent and beloved sovereign George III.
> This tablet was erected by Thomas Bruce, Earl of Ailesbury.'

A few months later after a stay at Longleat with the Thynne family George III paid a visit to Savernake accompanied by the Queen and three of the royal princesses. Their route took them through Devizes and Marlborough on Wednesday September 16 1789. There was great rejoicing in both towns with the boys from Marlborough Grammar School celebrating with much ringing of bells and drinking of beer. In honour of the King's arrival at Tottenham House Thomas tried to blow the great ivory hunting horn inherited from the Norman Esturmys, but to his embarrassment only a few squeaks issued forth.

The house itself had been altered and enlarged in the earlier years of the 18th century, "Capability" Brown had advised the laying of the grounds and forest walks, and wings had been added. The house acquired its final appearance in a complete remodelling and enlarging which took place between 1821 and 1856.

For many years the estate prospered under the wise management of several capable men, but it became financially strained under the extravagant rebuilding begun under the first marquess, Charles (1821 – 1856) and continued by his successor George Frederick (1856 – 1878). The years under the latter and his wife Mary Caroline of the Pembroke family are often considered the golden years of Tottenham House. The expanded Georgian house in warm golden stone was enormous and the interior was decorated and furnished lavishly with no thought for expense. It took two dozen servants and twenty gardeners to run it efficiently. But it proved to be too big and rapidly became a white elephant. George Frederick thought the outside of the house too plain so he added the stone lions which stand proudly over the arches and beneath each lion he added his monogram with the Garter encircling it. He also added the date 1870 quite prominently though in actual fact the mansion, except for the lions, had been completed about fifty years earlier.

In spite of some financial strain of which George Frederick seemed largely unaware, many improvements continued to be made in the estate and many provisions of a social nature were made for its people. Charles built the church at East Grafton, though falling masonry caused a fatal accident in which the heir George Frederick narrowly escaped with his life. Charles also built schools and began a programme of repair for many dilapidated cottages. His good works were continued by his successor. George Frederick had married Mary Caroline Herbert, daughter of the Earl of Pembroke of Wilton House. They were unfortunately childless but Mary Caroline became a Lady Bountiful working tirelessly to improve the lot of her tenants. She persuaded her husband to build schools including one at Tottenham where she herself gave lessons to the local children. She opened a training school at Durley where girls were trained in laundry and other housewifely arts, many of them no doubt graduating to work at the big house. She founded Savernake Hospital, endowing it as a cottage hospital for the local poor. It grew to a size and importance she could not have envisaged. Two churches stand within the confines of the forest. Both were built by Mary Caroline. Cadley, just off the Salisbury Road, is one of the little country churches that has failed to survive. Sad and forlorn, it is now used as a dwelling place and sometimes laundry can be seen draped over the gravestones. Its little satellite school too is abandoned. The other church, St. Katherine's is a beautiful church built close to Tottenham house and was Mary Caroline's memorial to her mother, the Countess of Pembroke. Mary Caroline, along with her husband is buried under a massive white marble cross surrounded by an inscribed curbing. Other members of the family are interred nearby and inside there is a handsome memorial brass in memory of George Frederick given by the clergy of his estates in Yorkshire and Wiltshire. Another very valuable undertaking by this charitable couple was the construction of many cottages, of the most up-to-date design of the day, so that the area around Savernake is blest with housing superior to that of the average village. But these good works cost a great deal of money, George Frederick himself lived in high style and the estate was beginning to feel the strain when it was inherited by his brother Ernest in 1878.

The new marquess was already an elderly man when he inherited the title and the estates. He was not knowledgeable about land management, and though well-intentioned he was burdened by a large difficult family and was obliged to support three dowagers in the style to which they were entitled. He followed two peers who had been over-spending for years. His oldest son predeceased him after years of spending recklessly in a lifetime of debauchery and the heir was his young grandson Willie whom he thoroughly spoiled and who followed in his father's footsteps as a rake and libertine. In order to pay the debts incurred by his son and grandson Lord Ernest was forced to sell the family estates in Yorkshire. This almost broke his heart and he died a very old and pitiable man. The title and estate passed to Willie who made no attempt to mend his ways. Desperate for money Willie tried to break the entail and sell Savernake, but after years of ligitation this proved unsuccessful. The estate faced ruin and the marquess was reduced to penury. He decided to cut down the forest trees and sell them for timber, but worn out by his excesses he died in 1894 still a young man before he could destroy the forest. Strangely enough the Savernake tenants mourned his passing.

His uncle Henry became the fifth marquess, and helped by his wife, he began a lifelong programme of restoration. He enlisted the help of his tenants and had the invaluable help of Edward Merriman of Marlborough as his agent. The marquess lived for years in a small house at Leigh Hill and did not return to live at Tottenham House till the financial situation had improved. From then on the family only occupied one wing of the great house. The outlying estates became productive once more and the forest itself, suffering from long neglect, was cleaned up and an on-going programme of reafforestation begun. It is said that this marquess increased the tree population of the forest by more than a million trees. He it was who was responsible for making the forest into the beautiful woodland I remember from my childhood. He generously allowed the public full use of the forest.

He was succeeded in 1911 by his son, a veteran of the South African War and holder of the D.S.O.. This was the marquess I remember. When I was a child he was an elderly man, shabbily but genteelly clad in tweeds, generally to be seen at the wheel of a very old car which boasted solid rubber tires. We would see him occasionally in Marlborough, marvel at his worn clothes, but recognize him instantly for the aristocrat he was. As a governor of the Grammar School he often officiated at the annual prize giving and I received several of my prizes at his hands. He would, I remember make a short speech urging us to work hard and live morally upright lives. He was generally accompanied on these occasions by his wife, a lady of statuesque build fond of large hats and colourful dresses. She reminded me of Queen Mary in her dignity and style. Sometimes we would see his two young grandsons Viscount Savernake and the Honourable Piers Brudenell-Bruce riding in the forest and the environs of Marlborough and the whole area was saddened at the tragic death of their mother in London. During the war it was this marquess who played host to the Americans as they gradually took over responsibility for the storage and disposition of ammunition in the forest. After the war, the marquess found that changing economic conditions made it impossible for him to continue his father's work of restoring the forest or to maintain the property. Many of the outer estates were sold, the forest leased to the Forestry Commission, Tottenham House rented to Hawtreys, a boys' preparatory school, and the marquess retired to Jersey. For the first time since Norman days the borough of Marlborough no longer had the paternal guidance of a noble family.

From the time my sister and I were very small children it was always fun to go "to the Forest". Many a Sunday afternoon my father would take us on long rambles, teaching us the names of the trees, plants, animals and insects and telling us something of the forest's long history. As we grew older we would go off with our friends for summertime picnic teas in the forest. May and I used to argue the relative beauty of the sections of the Salisbury and London roads that ran through the forest. I liked Salisbury Road better, going as it did through the little village of Cadley, past Big-Bellied Oak and the part of the forest just before Leigh Hill that was full of hawthorn trees. Sometimes we would drive past Tottenham House, its huge bulk just visible on the distant horizon and there was a patch of heath with gorse and heather on the Great Bedwyn Road that became a favourite picnic spot, and was close to woods that were carpeted with bluebells in spring. Sunday School outings were sometimes held in the great grassy glade in the depths of the forest known as Braydon Hook (or Oak) and the forest, naturally was a favourite haunt of courting couples.

I met my husband David Wharton at a dance in Marlborough on August 5 1943. He was an American, stationed in Savernake Forest and billetted in Tottenham House. A few days after we met he invited me to an American Officers' dance at Tottenham House. A group of Marlborough girls were picked up in a command car and driven through the gathering dusk of a beautiful summer evening to the front entrance of the great mansion where our escorts met us, and led us into one of the great reception rooms. Stripped in wartime of most of its furnishings, the beautiful proportions of the design of architect Thomas Cundy seemed more readily apparent. The girls were mostly attired in colourful dresses – finery left over from pre-war wardrobes. I remember I wore a black taffeta gown, its long full skirt appliqued with scarlet roses and emerald green leaves. Our partners were mostly young men, many newly commissioned and only a few weeks off the boat. They wore the wartime "dress" uniform of "pink" pants and olive tunics, the insignia of their rank shining on their shoulders. As we danced in the great room and strolled on the terrace overlooking grounds that had originally been laid out by "Capability" Brown, the war seemed very remote. It was as if we were in another place, another time. It was indeed a night to remember.

It can be said that we began our married life in Savernake Forest. After our Marlborough wedding and a honeymoon in London and Edinburgh, we spent a few weeks together, staying first at the Savernake Forest Hotel. This small hostelry had been built by the Marquess of Ailesbury to accommodate travellers arriving by train at

Savernake station en route for Marlborough. Built on the edge of the forest a stone's throw away from the station, its redbrick design clearly shows its relationship to what might be called early railway architecture. It remains today a charming little country hotel offering accommodation to those exploring the vicinity and good food to all comers. During the war it was a safe haven for the wives of men stationed in the vicinity and wealthy evacuees from London and other places at high war risk. It was the early summer of 1944 and my husband was working long hours seven days a week with troops assembling and readying for shipment ammunition hidden in the forest. He would generally put in an appearance in the early hours of the morning, throw a pebble up to my window and I would creep down to let him in, steeling myself to face the cockroaches which appeared every night in spite of the best efforts of the proprietors to get rid of the pests. The days were long and lonely and I would generally catch a train from Savernake to Marlborough to spend a few hours with my mother. Later we took a room in a house belonging to Mr Lionel Wootton, head deerkeeper for the marquess and one of the old retainers still in his employ. We did this largely in the interests of economy as David was at that time only a First -Lieutenant. The cottage was in Durley not far from Lady Wright's Riding School. As cottages go it was relatively spacious and we had a nice feather-bedded room up under the eaves. I took my meals in the big kitchen. Mr Wootton was a big beefy man with a strong Wiltshire accent and a huge walrus moustache. His wife was very quiet, rather small and grey-haired. She was an excellent cook in English country fashion and in spite of wartime restrictions seemed to have access to plenty of milk, butter, eggs and summer fruits and vegetables which came in quantity from the big garden. There was plenty of game and poultry too for her soups, stews and pies which were delicious. She seemed never to be out of her kitchen, which was very hot in summertime from her big black range and had a table in the centre where she seemed to be perpetually rolling pastry. Lionel appeared to have an insatiable appetite and in addition to me she had a young English officer's wife and child staying in the house. "Paddy" Sage and I spent D-Day together, listening to the constant drone of planes all day and wondering what it presaged for the war in general and for us in particular.

In the spring of 1985, in the company of Oscar Fulk and a visiting American from Ohio named Ralph Ricketts – he had been stationed briefly in Marlborough and had worked with Oscar at the old station – we ignored the Keep Out notices and drove up the long straight road through what had been the deer park to Tottenham House. Gaunt, huge and looking generally uncared for, though the lions still stand proudly aloft, one wing was ringed by scaffolding. A few workmen were going desultorily about their tasks. They ignored us completely. My husband, I suspect, tried to visualize it as he remembered it, alive with the business of Americans at war, but I tried to imagine it as it must have been on the occasions of two royal visits, that of George III in 1789 and the Prince and Princess of Wales, later Edward VII and Queen Alexandra nearly 100 years later. Then with lights, music, footmen, elegantly dresses ladies and gentlemen it was the scene of life in the grand manner – something that will never return to Tottenham House.

Chapter 4

THE VILLAGES

"But there were trim, cheerful villages, with a neat or handsome parsonage and the grey church set in the midst; cottages with bright transparent windows showing pots full of geraniums and little gardens all double daisies and dark wallflowers and towards the free school small Britons dawdling on . . ."

George Eliot

For all its changes Marlborough's character is unaltered – she is still a charming old market town, a local centre, still tied closely to the College, and because of her long history, her beauty and her wide street, she remains very attractive to tourists. The villages around have undergone more fundamental changes though at first glance they appear much as George Eliot described them over a hundred years ago.

Generally speaking, the sites of towns and villages are determined by water supply, so that in the Marlborough area we find villages along the Kennet and its tributaries, built, not in the flood plain, but on the chalk at its edge. They are small agricultural communities, some straggling along main roads, while others cluster in storybook fashion around their churches and village greens. Those easily accessible by good roads have grown large, while the more remote ones have remained small because of their isolation. The village is one of England's oldest institutions. A good water supply and good defensibility first brought man to settle in a particular place, but the village as we know it developed in the Middle Ages, a normal outgrowth of the feudal system of land tenure. Dwellings grew up around a lord's castle, a church was built, craftsmen plied their trades, agriculture was carried on under the three field system and each village developed into a self-sufficient independent community which had little concern with or interest in its neighbouring villages.

This state of affairs was to last many centuries, though there was an agricultural revolution in the 19th century. Real change began to come after World War I, change which was vastly accelerated by World War II and the economic and social changes of the succeeding years. While the appearance of the village, in spite of much growth, remains much the same, the character of the village has changed dramatically.

The villages are more prosperous today than ever before, and this prosperity is reflected in their trim neat appearance. Years ago, in spite of their idyllic semblance, many villages hid pockets of dire poverty. Apart from the squire, the parson, the doctor, a few gentlemen farmers and a handful of skilled rural craftsmen, the majority of the inhabitants were farm labourers, who were for many years on the lowest rung of the economic ladder. They lived in picturesque cottages, which often had no running water, no sanitation and lacked systematic repair. Families tended to be large, children were fed and clad inadequately and there was little prospect of breaking the cycle of poverty that was self-perpetuating. Labourers often lived in tied cottages, so that if they attempted a change in jobs they became homeless. Their condition depended for years on the character of two men in the village – the squire and the parson. Some of these cared for their tenants and parishioners in a spirit of noblesse oblige, but others had no such sense of responsibility. The village parson was sometimes a younger son of a landowner, a fox-huntin' man, the church for him a sinecure and such a man spent little time ministering to the physical or spiritual needs of his flock. Flora Thompson in *Lark Rise to Candleford* deplores the lot of the farm labourer at the same time she extols the beauty of the countryside. I know that my mother, brought up in villages, was very grateful to live in a small town even though moneywise she was not much better off, and in World War II as a teacher evacuated from Birmingham, I found much to deplore in village life. But modern times have brought prosperity to the villages and both population and living styles have changed tremendously. This has been due largely to modern methods of transportation and the opening up of the super highways. Once the M4 was completed the villages in the Marlborough area were within easy reach of London. Old cottages, many on the point of being condemned, were bought up by developers and business people and converted into weekend cottages or second homes, preserving their old world charm and adding all modern conveniences. Village housing also became popular for people working in nearby towns in business and professional capacities and much new building went on, some of it modest, some more luxurious, but most of it in keeping with the old. No longer is the population confined to those who work on the land, for now village residents are likely to come from many walks of life and from many disparate places, and though they live in the village they are unlikely to work there. Many of the young people from the old original village families, whether land owning or labouring, are leaving to seek their fortunes elsewhere, while those who remain to work on the farms are finding that agricultural work is upgraded and better paid than ever before.

There are however changes, very important ones though not at first sight visible. Many of the big houses – every village boasted several – are no longer the residences of the local landowners, who in many cases can no longer afford to keep them up. Some are hotels, some have been converted into flats, some are group homes, some are hospitals. The former manor may have become an ordinary working farm. The few big establishments that are run as they were in the old days most likely have been bought by the nouveau riche business tycoon or movie star. While for the most part the new inhabitants of the villages are proud of local landmarks, the village churches sometimes look neglected and rundown, their tombstones half hidden in unmown grass. With congregations shrinking, some have been closed while others operate on a rota basis with two or three neighbouring churches. Once one of the wealthiest bodies in the world, the Church of England is hurt by inflation and lack of interest in religion. There are a faithful few in every village who are loyal and work hard, but the task is often beyond them. The village school, a mandated institution since 1870 and often in existence for years before then is no more. The little buildings of pseudo-ecclesiastical design huddle in the shadow of their churches empty and abandoned for little Britons no longer dawdle to their doors, but are bussed to a central school in the nearest town. The institution which profits most from the changes in the village society is the inn or public house. It is thriving as never before. No longer is the village inn merely a place where weary farm labourers can enjoy a pint of the local brew – now in addition to a wide variety of beverages the inn serves snacks of all kinds and often gourmet meals. Once a "pub" under inspired management gets a reputation for good food and company, people from miles around will flock to it.

For years between the wars, many of the rural crafts of England began to disappear, giving way to mass production and automation. Since World War II there has been an attempt to revive them and many villages now boast thatchers, blacksmiths, ditchers and hedgers who reinforce their ancient skills with judicious use of modern methods. With the rise in popularity of thatch for roofing, thatchers in particular are much in demand. Wheat straw, once the prime material for Wiltshire thatch is now rarely used, since new ways of reaping render it useless for that purpose. Norfolk reeds replace it. Local craft fairs and much publicity in newspapers, magazines, on radio and television have stimulated interest in the revival of a priceless part of rural heritage.

Most villages have something unique in the way of history, prehistory or ancient customs and these are carefully preserved by old and new residents alike. Avebury is world famous for its prehistoric temple and has a fine manor house and church too. Littlecote, near Chilton Foliat, a beautiful village on the Kennet, is one of the finest Tudor houses anywhere to be found. It has a ghost story involving the murder of a newborn baby in a mysterious birth, was the scene of discussions between James II and William of Orange and a beautiful Roman mosaic has recently been uncovered there. Henry VIII brought Jane Seymour to Littlecote and the lovers carved their initials in one of the mansion's windows. East Kennet has its Long Barrow, forbidding burial chamber of early downland dwellers and remote Yatesbury, long before the Air Force took it over was the scene of smuggling activities which may have given rise to the legend of the Wiltshire Moonrakers, though Devizes challenges this claim. Cherhill was notorious for a gang of thieves and highwaymen, who working out of the Black Horse Inn, robbed and terrorized neighbours and strangers alike, performing their nefarious deeds naked the more easily to terrify and more importantly escape recognition. Coate outside Swindon was the home of Wiltshire poet and writer, Richard Jefferies and Rockley and Wolfhall figured in the machinery riots of the 19th century. Froxfield has beautiful almshouses, built and endowed for the widows of clergymen by the Duchess of Somerset in 1686, Broad Town has its Charity given by the same lady. Mildenhall was the site of Roman Cunetio and has a very interesting old church with high box pews and two three decker pulpits. Great Bedwyn also has a Norman church and a stonemason's yard worthy of Thomas Wolfe's descriptive powers. Its ancient town hall was removed from the village street some years ago. Woodborough has its bulb farm, a spectacular sight in the spring when the tulips are in bloom. We saw the fields in moonlight in 1985. Wilton has its windmill, Crofton its pumping station which made canal and engineering history and several villages and towns boast the white horses on the downs which are the very symbols of Wiltshire.

Compton Bassett has an ancient church with an unusual stone carved rood screen. It also has a beautiful manor house. In the thirties, this house and its estate were bought by a Mr Guy Benson and his wife Lady Violet Benson. She was a daughter of the Duke of Rutland and sister of Lady Diana Manners one of the great beauties of the time who married Mr Duff Cooper. Since Lavington and Hooper handled the sale and transfer of the estate to Mr Benson, my father went to Compton Bassett quite often for a time. Occasionally I went with him and I remember the lovely walled kitchen garden with espaliered peaches and nectarines. In the greenhouse I saw cherry tomatoes for the first time as well as a strange variety with yellow skins. In the 1950s, coincidentally, when I was boarding the Queen Mary at Southampton, the lady who was checking in immediately ahead of me was Lady Violet Benson. She was conducted to First Class accommodations while I was travelling tourist so I never saw her again either on board or when we disembarked in New York.

I am constantly amazed at the number of villages in the Marlborough area, no less than in other parts of England. There is a network of roads linking them and stretches of arable and pasture land and areas of woodland surrounding them. The typical village with towered or steepled church, a stream or pond, a green with flower bedecked cottages clustered around, the inn, the shop, the big house, the outlying farms – the scene is repeated endlessly, but with uncountable variations. The villages and small towns set in the fields and woods of the countryside comprise the England that poets have written about, that empire builders remembered in distant far-flung outposts, that soldiers fought for, that tourists want to see and to which expatriates like myself return whenever they can. Though change has come most of it is for the better for today rich and poor alike enjoy a high standard of living among some of the most beautiful country in the world.

Chapter 5

THE TOWN

"The more things change the more they stay the same."
French Proverb

Perhaps the question I was asked most often in 1985 was, "Has Marlborough changed?" Sometimes it was phrased differently, "What changes do you see in Marlborough?" The latter was easier to answer. Change is part of the very fabric of life, in fact history is the story of change, sometimes gradual and peaceful, sometimes sudden and violent. So my answer is, "Yes, I can see some significant changes in Marlborough in my lifetime and these changes are more apparent to me because I have spent many years away, even though my absence has been punctuated by relatively frequent visits back."

The beginnings of Marlborough are lost in the mists of time, but once written records were established it can be seen that her story is one of change which has continued to this day and will continue on into the future. Change is brought about by population growth, disasters such as fire and war, desire for improved living standards and different styles, introduction of new methods of transportation and Marlborough in common with the rest of the country has responded to them. One very great change took place in the early Middle Ages – indeed it gave birth to Marlborough as we know it today. A Saxon settlement had grown up around the open space we know today as the Green and later it became the parish of St. Mary's Church. A Norman community developed around the Mound and the castle the early Normans built atop it, and St. Peter's Church took care of their spiritual needs. Eventually the two settlements merged linked by the High Street, the very heart of Marlborough. The changes that have occurred within my memory have been brought about by rapid and diverse development in transportation, the variety of modern inventions, the two world wars, a growing

31

population and the increasing demands for better housing and living conditions.

The trick for old towns like Marlborough is to change what must be changed to keep up in a changing world, but to do it in such a way that the ancient character and fabric of the place is not destroyed. To preserve that is essential both for prosterity and present and future prosperity. People visit a town like Marlborough for its timeless charm and beauty and Marlborough's economy depends on maintaining them. It is my conclusion that the town has been relatively successful in the balance between necessary change and essential preservation. Marlborough, by virtue of its very wide High Street which has needed no change to accomodate the ever increasing amount of road traffic, is more fortunate than many old towns with very narrow, centuries-old streets. True, Marlborough does have problems because the roads leading in and out of the High Street are very narrow, and certain changes in traffic patterns have been made in an attempt to ease bottlenecks, which often cause delays at peak periods, but the width of the High Street itself is such that it can accommodate parking for many cars in its centre.

Remembering the High Street as I knew it when a child, and reinforcing my memories by studying *Marlborough in Old Photographs* by Michael Gray and Francis James, I think it has changed remarkably little. Repair, restoration, and adaptation have gone on apace, most, though not all, done with understanding and fidelity. Mr Gray says in the preface to his book that some changes have been made which should not have been, though others, mostly done by local builders and craftsmen have been executed with taste and sensitivity. He particularly criticizes the chain stores for what they have done to the fronts of many old buildings. Some years ago I heard much criticism levied at the red brick edifice of rather modern design put up by the Ramsbury Building Society, but it has mellowed with time and does not seem as obtrusive as it did at first. One very recent traffic modification measure has raised a storm of protest. The High Street pavement leading to Kingsbury Street has been built out into the roadway creating a bulge. It was put there in an effort to slow traffic as it approaches the hilly curve into Kingsbury Street and towards the Common. I did not find it offensive myself, but I did wonder if it would prove more hazard than help to drivers unaware of its existence. Changes such as these are always resisted at first, generally by older residents, and it must be remembered that time of itself brings an acceptance of change which at first may have offended and outraged many.

As I walk along the High Street, down the Parade and along London Road, I am saddened less by building changes than the fact that I see few stores bearing the familiar names of merchants of my childhood days; for sixty years ago I regarded them as permanent and changeless. Butchers, Dunford, Webber, Cooper, Searle and Bernard, grocers, Burchell, Pocock, Stratton Sons & Mead, hairdressers, Gillette and Archer, drapers, Sloper, Harraway, Jackson, Calvert and Say, dress shops such as Paris House and Jeanette's, bakers Hart, Knapton and Bernard, jewellers Collier and Chivers, chemists Gantlett and Baker, greengrocers Burgess and Neate, ironmongers, Milburn and Phillips, Dale and Pope, all, all are gone, replaced by strangers or taken over by chains. H. Duck, once a bicycle shop, now primarily a toy shop, is one of the few retaining a familiar name, and Owen Hurd's shoe store is, refreshingly, just the same. Stopping in to see the present proprietor, son of the man who fitted us with shoes for many years, I found the shop unchanged, narrow and dark, its walls lined with shoe boxes, but it was the smell of leather, combined with shoe polish and beeswax that took me back to those years when my mother went to Mr Hurd for our shoes. She liked the brands he carried, always buying the best her limited funds could afford. She believed he fitted shoes expertly and as no one else could. I learned from his son that his older brother Owen had died many years ago and that his sister, appropriately enough, had become a chiropodist. I remember those three children, contemporaries of ours, walking with their mother as we did with ours. Family shoe stores seem to have outlasted other family owned businesses for it was only recently that Mundy's closed following the untimely deaths of the owner Jim Mundy and his wife, the former Barbara Barcham.

Marlborough has always had plenty of restaurants. Her position on what was for many years the main London–Bristol road, and her wide street with plenty of shops and parking has made her a favourite stopping place for tourists and travellers. While the development of the public houses as eating places has cut into the restaurant business, there are still many in the town that do a brisk trade for breakfast, morning coffee and afternoon tea in addition to lunches and dinners. Some have been there for many years, though others are new to me. The Polly Tea Room is still Marlborough's preferred restaurant, though since a disastrous fire one Fair day it lacks its upper storey. It is many years since Miss Leith-Hay and Miss McCleod, elegant cultured ladies, opened and ran the restaurant with courteous efficiency, creating a gracious ambience and serving the finest food.

Some of the nice older private houses in the High Street have become places of business or have been demolished and replaced, and this I feel has been a loss to the street and to the town. The Priory is now a home for older people, and its beautiful gardens with shady trees, herbaceous borders and green lawns sloping down to the river have become a park, left to the town by Mrs Thomasine Clay in memory of her husband. Ivy House, at one time a private school for boys, is now a residential hotel. Waterloo House – its name indicates it was built shortly after 1815 – is now demolished. For many years the Marlborough Times was printed there. The paper was owned by a Mr Perkins, a dark handsome man who had lost a leg in the war. He had an attractive family which included twins. Beautiful Ashton House is now the Georgian restaurant. It was the home of a Mr Adams who owned a once famous brewery. The lanes and alleys off both sides of the High Street have been opened up and have become choice locations for residences. Some are new buildings, but others have been renovated, enlarged or combined. Those on the lower side of the street have gardens that go down to the Kennet. Some of the oldest buildings in town are to be found in these lanes, and charming houses with lovely walled gardens are tucked away there. During the Civil War, Royalist troops gained entry to the High Street down one of these, consequently named Horsepassage Lane. It is beside the White Horse Bookshop, a very old and beautiful building and was later known as Chandler's Yard, as it was ·the home of the first saddlery shop owned by the family of that name.

The churches at either end of the High Street and the Town Hall remain much the same. Though St. Peter's is no longer used as a place of worship, it serves a useful purpose as a community and tourist centre, and after much discussion relating to traffic flow, it was decided to retain one of its most distinctive features – its coffin-shaped churchyard which stands in the middle of the High Street at its western end. Traffic is barred from the very narrow road on the north, where there are some very old buildings, some residential, some shops, small and dark but with an air of ancient mystery. St. Mary's Church is the parish church of the town. It is approached from the High Street by a narrow covered walk called Patten Alley. In olden days it was a muddy lane, and ladies fitted iron rings called pattens to their shoes to keep them free from mire. From the Green the path to the church is lined with pollard lime or linden trees. They are unattractive in winter, with bare truncated branches ending in balls of twigs caused by the severe pruning of the pollard process, but in summer the green leaves burst out in such profusion that a green tunnel is formed. When the trees blossom they are alive with bees and the air is permeated with a delightful fragrance. The south side of the churchyard was converted into a park some years ago. Old gravestones were laid flush in the green turf, and paths and seats make it a good place for rest and contemplation. It has a good view of the edge of Savernake Forest. The land falls off sharply into New Road as it nears the High Street and a stone wall has been built for retention. There were ten dwellings on this steep land known as High Walls, but they were demolished in 1932 in one of the town's first efforts to eliminate sub-standard housing.

The former St. Peter's School is now the Public Library, while St. Mary's Infants' and Girls' School in Herd Street is now a private dwelling. The youngest children now go to a new school in George Lane, juniors, both boys and girls go to the building which for many years was Marlborough Grammar School, while students over the age of 11 go to St. John's School, first to the Savernake Building in Chopping Knife and later to the Stedman Building on Granham Hill in a comprehensive system of education.

One of the earliest housing estates to be built in Marlborough was St. John's Close. Just after the turn of the century three College masters bought a tract of land south-west of the Common and built houses on it to provide working people with improved housing. The land was part of the endowment of St. John's Hospital of medieval times, hence the name. There remained, however a desperate need for upgraded housing and in the twenties the Council built a group of low rent semi-detached houses between Blowhorn and Cold Harbour Lane. It was named Lainey's Close after a tenant of the land in the 17th century. Two more large housing estates were built between 1930 and 1936, Isbury Road and Cherry Orchard and others were built after World War II to ease the housing shortage that arose. Many small houses have been built and some formerly large houses converted for use by the town's elderly and it is my impression that Marlborough has every right to be proud of the way in which she has provided adequate housing for all income levels. New building is still going on. A group of upper middle class homes is being developed on the Bath Road, opposite the road leading to Manton. We drove around, noting the type of construction and comparing it with that which is going on in the States today. The prices shocked us. Property is very expensive in Marlborough, partly because of its desirability, and partly because very little land is left to develop. To the north lies the Common, to the west most of the property belongs to the College, while Savernake Forest is east and south of the town.

Population growth and demands for better housing are responsible for the explosion of building that has occurred in Marlborough. Though many new houses have been built, many old ones have been altered and renovated. The town will permit no changes in the exterior of buildings that are considered part of Marlborough's ancient heritage, though some unfortunately were altered before this ordinance came into effect. Changes in methods of transportation make for another factor that has brought alterations to the town. It was the twenties that saw a great rise in motor traffic. Many men had learned to drive in World War I and as soon as the economy had recovered sufficiently to make small cars within easy reach of the average wage-earner then the roads in summertime were filled with pleasure seekers. The old narrow streeted towns of England were faced with traffic problems of great magnitude. Marlborough had to face the difficulty of getting traffic in and out of her wide High Street, a problem which is still not fully resolved.

One of the first road changes I remember – undoubtedly because it was right where we lived – was where the Salisbury and London Roads come together. When I was very yong there was a triangular green opposite our house. This green was bounded by the London Road and the Salisbury Road which merged at the bridge across the Kennet, while on the east beyond our house the London Road split forming a road which crossed the Salisbury Road and became George Lane. This crossroads, known at that time as Polydor – why I do not know – was the scene of several accidents. Most were not serious as speeds were not high and most drivers exercised caution, but when one happened it was a source of great excitement and interest. Local householders, my father often among them, bystanders and passers-by would congregate, render assistance if need be and argue vocally and vociferously the merits of the case, often assigning the blame and generally helping or hindering the police with their opinions. Eventually this crossroads along with the green was eliminated and a modified circular flow of traffic was instituted, the two main roads converging opposite our house while the side road connecting with George Lane was dispensed with. The change certainly cut down on accidents and kept traffic moving, but it made for extremely hazardous pedestrian crossing. This concerned my parents when we were young and I remember worrying about my father trying to cross the road in his latter years of confusion and erratic behaviour. Without the green too the approach to the town was much less scenic. We used to play on the green when we were children and it made an impressive surround for the grey granite obelisk, flanked by World War I guns that was the town's memorial to the 7th Battalion of the Wilts Regiment. It had been erected in 1919 to the memory of 360 men who had died in the war. The hastily mustered battalion had trained in Marlborough in the early days of the war under Colonel Rocke. The men were billeted in the town and made many friends there. They served in Salonika from 1915–1917 and in France in 1917 and 1918, suffering heavy casualties. Now their monument stands forlornly on the south side of the London Road, barely noticed and well-nigh forgotten, black with the dust of passing traffic.

One of the greatest traffic problems today seems to be the ever increasing number of trucks and lorries that pass through the town and clog the roads approaching it. These great vehicles thunder along narrow streets shaking centuries old buildings to their very foundations, making conversation with friends on street corners impossible and causing walking, even on the pavement to be hazardous. It was thought that much traffic would be eliminated when the M4 bypassed Marlborough, but such does not appear to be the case.

If there are more lorries there seem to be less buses. The red double-decker Wilts & Dorset buses whose routes crisscrossed the area and linked Marlborough with its satellite villages, now operate on a very limited schedule and even the number of buses to Swindon are fewer than in years past. We loved to go to Swindon when we were children largely to visit Woolworth's and have lunch or tea at McIlroy's where Mother occasionally bought us clothes. More and more people travel to and from work by car and the two-car family is not unusual. Parking is always a problem and houses that front onto narrow streets cannot stand their cars outside their doors for a moment.

Marlborough's rail service was discontinued some years after the war and this of course put an added burden on the roads. Prior to the advent of the railway Marlborough was a very important centre of communication. By 1792 regularly scheduled coaches left several inns in Marlborough, several times a day and several times a week going to London, Bath and Bristol and intermediate towns. At the height of the coaching era 44 coaches a day called at Marlborough and royal mails regularly passed through the town at the unheard-of speed of 9½ miles per hour. Marlborough was a most important stop in the East–West route.

Early in the 19th century a short-lived, but for a time a very important means of communication came into being with the opening of the Kennet and Avon Canal in 1810. It did not touch

Marlborough. The peak of the canal's importance came in 1838, after which its use rapidly declined and it was purchased by the Great Western Railway in 1852. Between 1840 and 1843 the railway from London to Swindon was constructed by Isambard Kingdom Brunel. It bypassed Marlborough as the Ailesbury family opposed the suggestion that it should follow the Bath Road. Swindon developed rapidly and became the home of the Great Western Railway works. In 1862 a line from Hungerford to Devizes was opened but Marlborough was left with no main line railway connection nearer than Swindon 12 miles to the north and Savernake 5 miles to the south. Eventually Marlborough was connected to the railway at Savernake by a branch line. It was very difficult and costly to build because of steep gradients necessitating construction of a tunnel. The first engine, old and not very highpowered, was nicknamed the Marlborough Donkey, but the little private company that had undertaken the construction of the line proved very profitable. Later a direct line between Southampton and Cheltenham passed through Marlborough. This proved useful as a line of communication during the two World Wars and a small branch line on the edge of Savernake Forest served the American troops well.

Because of the canal and rail development the London–Bath road lost its importance as the coaches declined and Marlborough suffered a severe economic loss exacerbated by her tardy rail connections. What little road traffic there was did not go through the High Street and it was not until the first World War and the twenties that it returned. In order to attract it for economic reasons into the High Street, the Corporation in 1926 designated part of the street for use as a parking place for motorized vehicles other than lorries. It was a wise move. With the rapid growth of the College compensating for the economic loss Marlborough suffered from lack of railway connections, traffic returned to the very heart of the town and business began to boom.

Marlborough's rail service was discontinued some years after the war and this put an additional burden on the roads. Marlborough had had two stations, the High Level which was closed in 1933 and the Low Level which continued to operate until 1961 when all passenger services were withdrawn. Marlborough felt the loss of her railway connections keenly. The stations were always extremely busy at the beginning and end of the College terms and at those times there was a regular procession of boys and luggage to and from the stations. Many vehicles, motorized and horsedrawn, would be available and local boys would act as makeshift porters for a few coppers. A weekly cheap excursion ran to London and it was much used for trips "to town". Many of my contemporaries remember the excitement of going to London by train, of changing at Savernake and the bleak little stations that represented our gateway to the world. They were the scene of many joyful reunions and many poignant farewells. The Low Level Station was the hub of much military activity during the war. Oscar Fulk was the American Rail Transport Officer who kept operations running smoothly, receiving and dispatching men and material. But all that is left today of the old station is a flight of concrete steps leading to nowhere, while nearby are buildings that house a residential school for children with learning disabilities.

Change and then more change, with still more yet to come, was, is and will be Marlborough's story. The pattern can be seen very clearly in a brief recapitulation of her past history.

Ancient Britons and their successors, the Romans, the Saxons, the Normans all played their parts in formulating the town of Marlborough. The earliest people erected the Mound, the Romans settled at Cunetio nearby and their roads ran through the area, forming the first lines of communication, the Saxons built their first rude huts around the Green and the Normans built the castle atop the Mound which flourished under King John and his son Henry III. The castle fell into ruin during the Wars of the Roses, but by then the town was firmly established. It had been granted a charter by King John in 1204 and had grown up around its Norman churches, writing many of its own laws and establishing its own customs. Henry VIII's marriage to Jane Seymour brought it to royal notice once more and Edward VI chose it for the site of one of his schools. During the Civil War the town was a bone of contention between the Royalists and the Parliamentarians. Several bad fires partially destroyed the town, but Cromwell organised financial aid for its rebuilding. By virtue of her location on the main road between London and Bath, Marlborough prospered during the coaching era and was the location of several fine inns. She was hurt economically by the introduction of the railways which bypassed her, but this disaster was largely counteracted by the growth of the College and its development into one of the premier schools of England, bringing much trade and prosperity to the town. Marlborough again by virtue of her location tended to prosper during the two World Wars, though in common with the rest of the country she mourned the loss of many of the brightest and best of her youth. Since World War II, Marlborough has grown and is a thriving market town. Due to her beauty, history, location, identity with the College, the opening of the M4, Marlborough is a very desirable town for both residence and tourism. Though there is some disaffection among her youth and worry over unemployment, it seems less acute than in many other parts of the country.

Marlborough so far has been able to adapt to and capitalize on change and I have no doubt that with continued wise leadership, she will go on doing so whatever the future may hold.

Chapter 6

THE COMMON AND THE GREEN

"And the voices of children are heard on the green."
William Blake

Most probably the first settlements of the eastern part of Marlborough were in the Silverless Street area and around the Green. The
"open" fields were the acres of Portfield in the north and this was
unenclosed arable land till 1823. The Common or Thorns became
the pasture land of the community, where since the 13th century
cows, but not sheep, could be put out to graze. In Elizabethan times
rights to the Common were more clearly defined. No one could
keep more than two cows there and each beast cost 8*d*. a year with
the owner providing a day's board for the herdsman who collected
the animals each morning by blowing his horn. He gained access to
the Common through a street which in consequence of this custom
came to be known as Blowhorn. A workhouse was built in the
middle of the 19th century on land adjacent to the Common since
permission was refused to allow the common land to be used for
such a purpose. Likewise the town cemetery of 1850 had to be placed
without the bounds of the Common, for that was to be reserved
exclusively for communal cattle pasturage. A bull was provided for
servicing the cows and it was housed in a shed in Blowhorn. It was
not until 1904 that the keeping of a bull was discontinued. Wandering animals were placed by the herdsman in a pound, a stone-
walled circular construction, standing near the pond in the south
west corner of the Common. I can remember this pound and pond
quite clearly. The pond was at best an inadequate water supply and in
dry weather the animals had to be driven to the river. Later the uses
to which the Common might be put were modified to include
games, athletic contests and races. The sheep fairs were transferred
from the High Street to the Common in 1893 and held there almost

continuously ever since and occasional agricultural shows were set up there. I can remember being taken as a child to the bonfire and fireworks show held on the Common on Guy Fawkes Day. During World War I some military manoeuvres were held there and German prisoners were housed in makeshift buildings. In the second war, the Americans established a hospital on the Common and later the Secondary Modern School used their huts until a permanent building was constructed. The Common is the site of a golf course and clubhouse, but otherwise remains an open bleak stretch of rough grassland leading to the open downs. At its northern end there is the tumulus, now almost denuded of the larch trees which formerly crowned its eminence and gave it the name of the Clump.

The other "open" space is the Green – thought to be the nucleus of the first Saxon settlement. In 1867 complaints were made about its general untidiness but because the church and the Marquess of Ailesbury both disclaimed responsibility nothing was done for some years. Eventually the posts and the chains were restored, grass reseeded, paths dug up and the trees pollarded and pruned. The Green ringed with old Tudor and Georgian houses with hidggledy-piggledy roof lines and dominated by the great grey pillared house that used to belong to the Elverson family, remains in my opinion one of the most attractive areas in Marlborough. I had plenty of opportunity to view it in my childhood for the way to St. Mary's School led steeply through the Green.

Various other open sites on the periphery of Marlborough were let out in allottments for Marlborough's gardeners. Much of the land for this was provided by the Marquess of Ailesbury and it seemed in a sense a modern continuation of the strip field system of land use and distribution. It was a common sight in my childhood to see part-time gardeners setting out on summer evenings with spades and forks over their shoulders to make use of the long hours of daylight. They would often return with baskets full of the fruits of their labours. It was traditional that the gardening season opened on Good Friday, which was a public holiday, and many British working men would do the preliminary spade work on that day.

Chapter 7

THE CHURCHES

"I like a tower.
It speaks of strength, of might, of power,
An emblem of the Church's strength
To overcome the world at length."
John E. Woodrow

All three of the Marlborough churches possess towers – strong sturdy ones. Two stand sentinel at either end of the High Street, the third to the westward beside the limpid waters of the River Kennet. Though the role of the church may have changed in the world of today and her present strength debatable, yet the towered buildings remain symbolic of the great faith out of which Western civilization grew. And when one wishes to delve into the history of a town, it is always well to look early at the churches, past and present, and of all denominations, for in the religious practices of a people history is writ large.

There are three churches in Marlborough of the Anglican persuasion, St. Mary's which is the Parish church, St. Peter's which, unfortunately, was declared redundant some years ago, and St. George's, Preshute, parish church of a wide area wandering erratically around the town proper. None of the present buildings are exceptionally old, though they are built on foundations of great antiquity and all present some interesting architectural features and historical memorabilia.

When the Saxons formed the first settlement around the Green somewhere around the 5th century, there is little doubt that they built a church on or near the site of the present St Mary's. A church is mentioned as being there in the Domesday Book, the chronicle of William's Norman conquest. It is believed that a larger Norman church replaced this one in the 12th century. All that remains of this

43

church, for it was burned down about 1460, is the fine round-arched heavily dog-toothed Norman door in the west wall of the tower, a pillar at the north-east corner of the tower and some corbels or stone brackets identified as being of Norman workmanship. In Tudor times the church was entirely reconstructed, a chapel was added at the east end and large perpendicular windows inserted. The tower, plain, sturdy and well-proportioned was built in the reign of Henry VIII. During the Civil War, when Marlborough was besieged and stormed, a band of Parliamentarian soldiers under Colonel Ramsay took refuge in the church and it came under heavy fire. Bullets and shot marked the tower and belfry. In 1653 the worst of several fires devastated Marlborough, flames caught the roof of the church and gutted the interior leaving only the outer shell. The church, with financial aid from Oliver Cromwell was rebuilt within a year, but the new interior was vastly different from what had been destroyed. It was of Puritan design, very plain and simple, with no stained glass and an absence of ornamentation. Though certain decorative additions have been made since, St. Mary's remains basically a fine example of church architecture and design of this period and few can help but admire the beauty of its plain uncluttered lines, its flat ceilings, unadorned arches and classical pillars. Needed repairs were carried out in 1844 when new pews were installed, and some thirty years ago a major restoration was completed.

One of the oldest relics in the church is thought to be a figure of the Roman goddess Fortuna. It was probably found at Cunetio and incorporated into the church at the time of the Tudor rebuilding. A Marlborough legend has it that one of the gargoyles is a representation of a heroic cat who lost her life rescuing her kittens in the great fire. There is a fine organ in the church which possesses excellent acoustical properties, and a ring of ten bells, the original eight augmented by two from St. Peter's. The white-faced clock with clear black figures was installed in 1888. Since it can be seen from most parts of the town it can be said to keep Marlborough punctual and it certainly got me to school on time for many years.

The church of St. Peter and St. Paul at the western end of town was undoubtedly built to take care of the Norman community which sprang up around the castle built on the Mound. The present church was built around 1460 and possesses a fine vaulted stone roof which was completed a few years before Thomas Wolsey, future cardinal and chancellor of England was ordained in the church in 1498. It is thought that some stones from the castle were used in the church's construction. Though the church escaped the great fire which destroyed St. Mary's, its tower bears the marks of shot and shell from the bombardment of the town in the Civil War. In 1862 a major restoration was undertaken by architect Thoman Henry Wyatt. While it is true to say he saved St. Peter's, it is also true to say he destroyed much in the church that was worth preserving. After World War I the south chapel was restored as a Lady Chapel as a memorial to parishioners who fell in that conflict. A similar chapel is in St. Mary's and the names of the World War II dead have been added in both churches. In St. Peter's there is a stained glass window in memory of those in the 7th Wilts Battalion who fell in the first World War.

There are some interesting memorials in St. Peter's. One is to James White who was innkeeper of the Castle Inn. It bears the date 1787. An earlier and sadder one commemorates Sir Nicholas and Lady Mary Hyde who in a 1626 epidemic lost their three young children. Sir Nicholas was Lord Chief Justice of England in the early years of the Stuarts. Set in the floor of the Lady Chapel is a stone to the memory of a physician who lived to the ripe old age of 108 and a brass memorializes Robert Weare seven times mayor of Marlborough. A boy named Fuller who attended the College in its earliest years is buried in the walled churchyard which surrounds the church in the middle of the street. Some consider it to be in the shape of a coffin and as such something of a rarity. The father of the notorious Dr. Henry Sacheverell was rector of St. Peter's at the time of his birth. He was born in the Rectory and baptized in the church.

Certain quaint bell ringing customs, discontinued now for many years, in both churches are worth mentioning. A Matin Bell used to be rung at St. Peter's every morning at 5. A curfew was sounded at 8 p.m. and a bell was rung at 12 noon on Shrove Tuesday which came to be known as the Pancake Bell. The Knell or Passing Bell was tolled at each church to announce the death of a parishioner. I can remember listening to this bell and counting the final tolling which indicated the age of the deceased. For many years a bell was rung every night at 9 p.m at St. Mary's. A traveller once lost on the downs was guided to Marlborough by the ringing of the bells at St. Mary's. In gratitude he left money to pay for a bell to be rung nightly to help benighted wayfarers in like circumstances. The custom ceased in 1914.

In 1917 the parishes were amalgamated and St. Peter's was not used for services for several years prior to its closure in 1976. It serves a useful purpose as a community centre and remains an architectural plus for the town.

Preshute Church is a tiny church on the western outskirts of the town. It is a church without a village though Manton is close by. Its parish is very old and very large and the church obviously served a widely scattered area long before Marlborough or its castle existed. The name "Preshute" was thought at one time to be a corruption of the Norman French "pres chateau" – near the castle, but now the preferred explanation is that it refers to the priest's "clete" or "cottage". The original church was most likely small and primitive and the priest a poor man. The present building dates only from 1854, though the tower may be considerably older. Its small but solid architecture with its squared flint work fits in well with its location at the foot of the downs and on the bank of the river. In fact it is an exceptionally attractive church set in its green churchyard among its ancient tombstones. It possesses a remarkable font, very old, very large, made of black marble quarried in Belgium. It most probably was brought to Preshute from the castle chapel of St. Nicholas, which was served by the Preshute priest, and it was in this font when it was in the chapel that the children of King John were most likely christened. There are also two very old brasses dated 1518 in the church, memorials to John Bailey and Maryon his wife. He was the Barton farmer of the time and his son later became vicar of Preshute.

The parish of Preshute covers an unbelievably large area and it appears to wander erratically around the town. We, living in London Road, well within the boundaries of the town, were in Preshute parish. Occasionally of a summer evening we would walk the fields to Preshute for Evensong, but our somewhat sporadic church going and Sunday School attendance was generally at St. Mary's. I was confirmed and married in that church though my parents and sister are buried at Preshute.

Down through the ages one of the most important parishioners at Preshute would have been, like the John Bailey of the brasses, the Barton farmer. Barton Farm, its entrance and house lying off the Bath Road opposite the College entrance was originally the Castle Farm. Its very ancient barn with a fine timbered roof was rebuilt in 1722, but unfortunately destroyed by fire in 1976. The farm now appears to have been taken over by the town and is the site of Marlborough's new, large and up-to-date swimming baths, but in my childhood it was farmed by a well-to-do family named Edwards. Mr Edwards was a handsome man, and Mrs Edwards a pleasant motherly looking lady who seemed to exude competence. There were several children among them two girls who were about the same age as my sister and myself. They were sometimes to be seen with their Nanny driving around town in a pony and trap. The girls I thought were very pretty, one blond and blue-eyed, the other dark with a piquant pixieish face. One of them died when a young married woman and once when I was in Preshute churchyard I saw a rosebush planted by her parents in her memory. I was deeply moved and I thought how strange it was that I should be so touched at the death of someone I scarcely knew.

As early as 1200 the extent of Preshute parish began to cause some problems. Marlborough had begun to expand eastward towards Ramsbury in an area called Newland. It was in the parish of Preshute, but the people soon began to complain about the distance from that church when St. Mary's was so close. A new chapel for their use was built and it was dedicated to St. Martin. It was in use from 1256–1549, but is no longer in existence. The name is preserved in the street known as St. Martin's and an old yew tree near the top of Poulton Hill marks the site where the chapel stood. When I was at St. Mary's School one of our teachers walked us down to the yew tree and told us the story of the old chapel and later we had to write an account of what we had learned. I have since thought what a marvellous way it was to learn history.

Other religious houses dating from the Middle Ages were in existence in Marlborough and area for varying periods of time. There was the Chantry House in the High Street, St. Margaret's, a Gilbertine Monastery in Salisbury Road, the Templar House near Rockley, the White Friars' Priory in the High Street, the Hospital of St. John which later became the Grammar School in the Parade and a leper hospital dedicated to St. Thomas off what is now Stonebridge Lane.

The Anglican churches were largely responsible for primary education in Marlborough, sketchy though it was before laws made it compulsory. There were 4 Sunday Schools in the town by 1788, each catering to about 30 children. A School of Industry was established for girls in 1811 and a National School was held in a building on the site of the old cinema, St. Mary's Infants' School was opened in 1850, St. Peter's Boys' in 1854 and St. Mary's Girls' in 1860. The curriculum was largely devoted to the three Rs and Religious Knowledge and Church dogma, doctrine and history was taught with the local parson generally shouldering some of the burden of the teaching. Even after the schools became state supported the church continued to contribute financially to their upkeep in return for retaining the right to teach doctrine. It was however not mandatory for pupils of another denomination to attend such classes.

The Chapel of Marlborough College is a vey beautiful building which stands on the west of the main entrance to the school. Dedicated to St. Michael and All Angels it is built of Sarsen stone in late Decorated style and is graced with a slender spire. It was opened in 1886. Marlborough College had originally been founded as a school for the sons of clergymen, and such applicants were given preference for many years.

There is a Methodist Church in New Road and the United Reformed Church once the Congregational Church is in the Parade. These buildings were opened by their respective members on 1816 and 1817, but they have been enlarged and improved since those days. Prior to these dates there had been several meeting houses in Marlborough the earliest founded in 1706, and a later one in Back Lane.

The history of the Nonconformist movement in Marlborough is an interesting one for a small town. When the Act of Uniformity was passed in 1662 requiring all Anglican ministers to subscribe to an oath of loyalty, certain preachers refused to swear, among them several ministers of some note in the locality of Marlborough. William Hughes, vicar of Marlborough, was one of them and in consequence he was deprived of his living. He remained in the town and continued to hold nonconformist meetings, even when it became hazardous to do so. His followers formed a sizeable and very dedicated minority. A pamphlet entitled *The Conversion of Mary Hurle*, chronicling the religious experiences of the daughter of a Marlborough glover had a wide circulation and influence locally. In 1706 a meeting house was built by a group of dissenting families, among whom were numbered such names as Merriman and Foster, prominent people in the community. The first years of the new meeting house were disturbed and the local conflict was exacerbated by the London disturbances between Dr. Sacheverell, born and educated in Marlborough, and Daniel Burgess who had preached in the town from 1674–1685. Both men were outstanding fiery preachers and their bitter rivalry led to the burning of Burgess's new meeting house in London. From 1711 to 1714 there was much civil disturbance in Marlborough when 'Presbyterians, Anabaptists and Independents' were in conflict with the established Anglican Church. At this time, Marlborough even had rival mayors. The conflict weakened and split the Nonconformists, but after a period of indecision a revival came when a new chapel with Matthew Wilks as minister was opened in Back Lane. Rowland Hill, one of the great national leaders of Nonconformity came to Marlborough and preached on the Green, but was pelted with stones and eggs. Hill, however introduced to Marlborough the greatest of her Nonconformist ministers, a man named Cornelius Winter. In addition to his ministerial duties, he opened a small boarding school and among his pupils was William Jay destined to become an outstanding minister and orator. This very young man left Marlborough in 1788 to go to London to preach under Rowland Hill, and large crowds went to hear him, attracted by his youth and vigorous discourse. But a split remained among Marlborough's non-conformists which weakened the movement as two rival factions developed. At first the nonconformists had attracted well to do professional men, but largely because of harsh laws which affected their livelihood, these gradually returned to the Anglican Church and nonconformity became basically a poor man's church, though some of the leading tradesmen of the town continued to support it. When finally the Marlborough Independents built their church in the Parade in 1817, William Jay, by now an old man, was invited to preach the inaugural sermon. Having begun his ministry in Marlborough he had gone to London and thence to Bath where he had served with great distinction for many years. It was not until 1821 that the Marlborough church was able to afford a resident minister, but it has continued to grow steadily ever since and made many improvements and enlargements of its first facility. Even though John Wesley himself had preached in Marlborough in 1745 and again in 1747, the Methodists remained poor and did not build till 1816 on a site in New Road. Religiously the town was divided into "church" and "chapel", this division quite apparent to me when I was growing up.

There were only a few Roman Catholics in Marlborough when I was a child. Most of these were Irish people who had some connection with the local stables training racehorses. After the Reformation in the 16th century, it was a crime to be a Catholic but a dedicated few used to meet in secret in the Hermitage in Hyde Lane. When religious intolerance ceased, Marlborough Catholics had no church to go to nearer than Swindon or Devizes. A chapel was built at Ogbourne Maizey in 1915 through the generosity of racing stable owners and trainers, Pat Hartigan chief among them. In 1937 Father Anthonioz came to Marlborough, the first resident Roman Catholic priest in the town for some four hundred years. He opened a small chapel in Elcot Lane prior to building the present church in George Lane on the site of the old George Inn. The church, an attractive modernistic building is dedicated to St. Thomas More.

The church calender dictated the life of the town to a very large extent. The school terms and holidays centred around Christmas,

Easter and Whit and half holidays were given on certain saints' days
and Ascension Day. Rates and taxes were due quarterly, the March
Quarter Day known as Lady Day which was the Feast of Annunci-
ation and the September one as Michaelmas Day which was the Feast
Day of St. Michael. Church attendance was compulsory for many
years for the Grammar School boys. There has been a revival in the
churches of certain ceremonial services which are attended by the
Mayor and Corporation in full regalia. It is quite an impressive sight
to see the procession headed by the Mayor in his scarlet ermine
trimmed robe followed by the black garbed Council members and
preceded by the Town Crier and the Mace Bearers. The Marlborough maces, made of silver gilt are very fine. Made in London in
1652 they bear the badges, mottoes and arms of the Commonwealth,
but after the Restoration of the monarchy, the king's arms and a
Crown were superimposed. One old church connected custom that
still survives – in fact it has been revived in recent times and is now
an annual event as it was originally – is the Beating of the Bounds.
On Rogation Day, which comes immediately after Ascension Day in
the church calender, a band of townsfolk, mostly young people,
walk around the boundaries of the town, striking the boundary
stones with sticks. In days when written records were scarce and
when reading and writing skills were minimal or non-existent, it was
a way of imprinting the outer limits of a place on people's minds.
Today it is purely ceremonial, a nice preservation of a past custom.

The non-conformists in Marlborough are now united and call
themselves the Methodist and United Reformed Church. They hold
their services in the New Road church now called Christchurch.
Marlborough is an ecumenical parish. There is one parish magazine
for all denominations, including Roman Catholics, known as *Tower
and Town* and several combined services are held each year.

Chapter 8

TWO SCHOOLS

"And then the whining school-boy, with his satchel
And shining morning face, creeping like snail
Unwillingly to school."
William Shakespeare

"We swing ungirded hips,
And lightened are our eyes,
The rain is on our lips,
We do not run for prize."
Charles Hamilton Sorley

Much of Marlborough's history is also the history of two schools, Marlborough Grammar School and Marlborough College, for the fame and fortunes of both are closely interwoven with the story of the town.

While today Marlborough Grammar School is a state supported secondary school serving the Marlborough area as hundreds of similar schools serve their districts all over the country, it was not always so, for its establishment as a school for boys took place in Tudor times. Marlborough College on the other hand is of comparatively recent origin. The long history of the Grammar School shows a generally steady if uneven rise in popularity and prestige as a school for boys, boarders as well as day pupils from 1550 until about 1860 when it began to deteriorate until 1899 it closed its door for six years, ultimately reopening as a co-educational school, state supported, for local pupils of academic ability which was determined by competitive examination. The College, founded as a boarding school for the sons of clergymen in 1843, after a shaky start forged ahead so that it rapidly became one of the premier schools in England, trailing only a shade behind such educational bastions of wealth, privilege

51

and ability as Eton, Harrow, Winchester and Rugby. The reversal of the respective schools' fortunes is what makes the story of the rival establishments so interesting.

On October 18th 1550 Edward VI gave sufficient money to the borough of Marlborough to build a Grammar School for boys. The appointment of the Master was vested perpetually in the head of the Somerset family, then wardens of Savernake Forest and closely related to the king through his mother Jane Seymour. The school first met in the medieval buildings of the former Hospital of St. John the Baptist situated in what used to be known as the Marsh and is now the Parade. Some twenty years later a new building was erected on the site. The curriculum was medieval, the boys receiving a thorough grounding in Latin Grammar with instruction in the writing of themes and mastery of rhetoric. The school continued small but satisfactory and fortunately its buildings were untouched by the fire of 1653.

In 1676 the Savernake estates passed from the Seymours to the Bruces when Thomas, Earl of Ailesbury married the Seymour heiress. There is a tradition that Thomas had attended Marlborough Grammar School as a boy, and from that time on the fortunes of the school were very much in the hands of the Ailesbury family. Under the will of Sarah, Duchess of Somerset in 1686 scholarships at Brasenose College, Oxford and St. John's College, Cambridge were endowed for boys from the school and additional endowments came from a widow, Jane Brown, who was related to the Somerset family. This further close connection with the Ailesburys formed the basis for the future development of the school and formed a link with the universities of Oxford and Cambridge unusual for a small provincial school.

The next fifty years saw a battle for power between the masters of the school and the town itself, for the mayor and council were reluctant to spend money on improvements, but a succession of strong masters raised its reputation over a wide area and developed it into a boarding school of some note as well as serving the needs of the town and immediate locality. Perhaps at this time the school's most distinguished pupil was Henry Sacheverell. He was born in 1673 in St. Peter's Rectory, the third son of the rector. From the Grammar School he proceeded to Magdalen College Oxford, where he took Holy Orders and formed a lifelong friendship with Joseph Addison, a fellow Wiltshireman. Sacheverell's strong vitriolic sermons in support of the Tories led to his impeachment in 1709. He was suspended from preaching for three years and his sermons were burned, but he achieved his objective for the Whig government fell.

During the following years Marlborough Grammar School pupils went into the Church and the professions in large numbers, serving for the most part with distinction. In 1809 a man named James Townsend Lawes became master. He had been educated at Warminster Free Grammar School and later became a teacher there where he had as one of his pupils Thomas Arnold, the future head of Rugby, an outstanding educator and father of the poet Matthew Arnold. Lawes was a strict and at times a brutal disciplinarian. The student body at this time seemed to separate into three distinct social classes, the boarders, a group of day boys belonging to prominent and wealthy local families such as the Merrimans and the Maurices, and the other town boys who were generally poor, dirty and ill-clad. Lawes, though a prominent and well liked man in Marlborough was a particular tyrant to these latter boys. He was the last old type master and under him the curriculum remained purely classical. At his death he left the school a handsome bequest. He was followed by Thomas Meyler under whose wise leadership the school reached its zenith. His strict but fair discipline helped restore the moral tone that the school had lost under the harshness of Lawes and he was much loved by his boys. On his death in 1852 the boys placed a stained glass window to his memory in St. Mary's Church and he is buried in the churchyard there.

During the tenures of Lawes and Meyler the school faced competition from other schools in the town for the first time. A school in the building in the High Street which is now Ivy House, was opened in 1780 by a Mr Davis who was followed by his son–in–law Mr Gresley. In 1804 the boys from this school cut the white horse on Granham Hill and it is most likely that two of Marlborough's most famous sons, brothers Thomas and Walter Hancock, of India rubber and steam engine fame respectively, attended this school rather than the Grammar School. There was also a school in Ramsbury under the leadership of Edward Meyrick that attracted many pupils away from the Grammar School. A descendant of this Meyrick later became an assistant master at Marlborough College and a noted biologist. He lived in a house called Thornhanger which faced the Common.

But the greatest competition of all was to come in 1843 when the Reverend Charles Plater opened Marlborough College in what had previously been the Castle Inn. Mr Meyler graciously welcomed the College to the town in a speech given at a dinner at the Ailesbury Arms in 1843, but he must have recognized that the College would be a considerable threat to the educational dominance that the Grammar School had so far enjoyed.

Marlborough College in its almost 150 years has had a tremendous influence on the town. It is true to say that without the College Marlborough would have been as any other little country town and it is the College which has brought economic prosperity and the advancement of academic and intellectual thought and cultural opportunity.

Though the school itself is of comparatively recent foundation yet the nucleus of its builing and its site reach far back into antiquity. Prior to the school's birth in 1843 the site had been a prehistoric mound, a Norman castle, a Tudor house, a Georgian mansion and a famous coaching inn. Its beginnings as a school were fraught with uncertainty, plagued as it was by financial difficulties and disciplinary problems. However with the appointment as headmaster of Dr. Cotton, both pupil and teacher at Rugby and disciple of Dr. Arnold, Marlborough began a long and successful growth as a noted public school, pioneering educational thought and practices under a series of brilliant masters, and staffed by outstanding scholars and teachers in their fields.

At first the town did not welcome the College. But with the decline of coaching and the fact that the railways bypassed the town, Marlborough faced economic problems. The town had lost much trade and the College soon proved a compensatory asset to offset the decline. In 1853 the Marquess of Ailesbury, hereditary governor of the well-established Marlborough Grammar School, proposed a scheme to unite the two schools with the College offering a classical education, while the Grammar School would concentrate on the science and business disciplines. The town raised a storm of protest and at a stormy public meeting voted it down decisively. Eighteen years later the suggestion was again put forward but this time it was the College, which had grown considerably in prestige in the interim, that refused to consider such a plan. One wonders what effect such an amalgamation would have had on both schools and town. Certainly the College would have gained a claim to a long history as an educational establishment and the town boys would have been assured of a broader education, but it was not to be.

For some years the two schools co-existed and there was some exchange and communication as well as friendly rivalry between the two. One college master, Mr Bond, became the master of the Grammar School for a brief period, and the school flourished for a while under his rule, but in the main there was a slow deterioration in the status of the ancient school. Dissatisfaction with the curriculum arose in the town and there was discussion on change but what little was resolved seemed to be counter-productive. The school closed in 1879 to open under a new regime two years later, but this was not successful. The school attracted no boarders, became purely local, the standard of work dropped and its connection with the universities and the professions was broken. The school struggled on for a few more years, expanding the technical side of education, but in 1899 it closed and remained so for six years. It was never again to be the type of school envisaged by its founders.

In 1902 legislation had been passed mandating the provision of secondary education for all pupils of both sexes who were deemed sufficiently able to benefit from it. Modest fees were to be paid by those who could afford it, but education would be free for those who could not. A new building was erected on the old site and the school opened in 1905 under Mr Sidney Pontefract. There were 80 pupils, the majority boys, for people, especially the parents of girls, were still suspicious of co-education. On into the nineteen-thirties there was a private school in the town that catered to the educational needs of girls. When my sister failed to get into the Grammar School Mr Meek of Marlborough High School came to see my mother with a view to admitting May there, but Mother came to the reluctant decision that she could in no way afford the fees. In 1928 I was fortunate enough to win a free place in the Grammar School. The school, in view of its ancient heritage retained the title of Grammar School and chose as its crest a representation of Marlborough Castle along with the date 1550. The most distinguished pupil of these years was without a doubt William Golding, winner of the Nobel Prize for literature and author of many novels, the best known of which is *Lord of the Flies*. He was the son of A.A. Golding well-loved science master at the school for many years. The pupils of my day were proud of the school's origin and under Mr A.R. Stedman who succeeded Mr Pontefract in 1932 we learned more about them and many old traditions were revived. The ancient scholarships were still available for those who could qualify. Considerable additions to the existing building coincided with Mr Stedman's arrival and plans were made for a new building on another site in view of increased demand and numbers. It was long delayed by the war and its aftermath but in 1961 the new building on Granham Hill was completed. After 411 years the Grammar School left the site where it had begun and in 1975 bowing to new educational trends it went "comprehensive", its student body comprised of all the children of Marlborough and its immediate district.

Marlborough College, in contrast to the Grammar School, steadily continued to grow in fame and fortune, its student body drawn from the rich and privileged from all over the country, and its graduates contributing to England's business, professional and service leaders. By 1870 it was in the front rank of England's public schools. Not only did the town gain economically and her tradesmen prosper because of the College, but the name Marlborough became known throughout the country as Old Marlburians distinguished themselves in many fields. The College has been responsible for much of the building that has gone on in Marlborough in the last hundred years. The boarding houses along the Bath Road were established from 1861, a sanatarium was built, a Natural History Museum opened. The lovely College chapel was completed in 1886 and a Memorial Reading Room marked the golden jubilee of the school. The old town gaol was converted and expanded into the gymnasium and the brick archway over the Bath Road, a notable landmark, was completed in 1911. The Memorial Hall was built in honour of the 750 Old Marlburians who gave their lives in World War I. The presence of the College has raised the standard of residential building, particularly in Marlborough's west end, and additional building continues. The beautiful and extensive playing fields are north of the town and west of the Common.

The staff too have influenced the town greatly and have added rich talent to the cultural life. Many masters have been active in town government and other phases of town life. Two assistant masters moved to the Grammar School, one, Mr Bond to be headmaster, another Mr Featherstone to be chairman of modern studies. College masters sat on the governing board of the older school. Local historical, antiquarian and natural history studies were carried on by College masters. The College has influenced the town's politics and adult education programs and the College Cadet Corps contributed many young officers in the two wars and joined in the Home Guard's defense efforts. During the war the College shared its educational facilities with the City of London School, the evacuated boys being boarded with the townspeople.

In 1968, in keeping with modern theories of education, the College admitted a small number of highly qualified girls and this has continued, though boys far outweigh the girls in number. More local pupils gain entrance as more scholarships are made available. The College becomes increasingly more active in the affairs of the town, becoming more involved in local government and sharing its academic and athletic facilities generously. Many Marlborough people are employed by the College in a variety of capacities. No longer is the very proper uniform of striped trousers, black jackets and Eton caps de rigueur. The boys wear an assortment of casual clothing which renders them largely indistinguishable from the town lads. Their upper class accents remain, however, contrasting with the soft slow Wiltshire dialect of the townspeople.

The great barn at Wolfhall, where tradition has it that Henry VIII and Jane Seymour danced at their wedding in 1536. It burned in 1960.

Marlborough High Street in 1985; looking east towards the Town Hall and St. Mary's Church. The Ailesbury Arms is on the right.

On the edge of Savernake Forest, near the entrance to the Grand Avenue, in 1985.

The Grand Avenue, Savernake Forest at the beginning of the war.

The mill, about 1936. It has been demolished, the land drained and built on now.

David Wharton with Oscar Fulk in Savernake Forest in 1944.

War Years American Style. Nissen hut on Postern Hill 1943.

Tottenham House in 1985. Americans were billetted here during the war; it is now a private boys school.

My sister's class of St. Mary's Girls School, Marlborough 1925. May is second left, back row.

The river Kennet at the bottom of our garden when I was a child.

Sgt. and Mrs Bill Nutley on their wedding day.

Sgt. and Mrs Oscar Fulk (nee Joan Head) in Savernake Forest in 1944. They lived briefly in the U.S. after the war, but returned to Wiltshire as landlords of the Red Lion at Axford.

Wedding group at reception in the Merlin Tea Rooms, 15 March 1944.

Bowood, near Calne, ancestral home of the Marquess of Lansdowne. Visited on VE-Day 1985.

My brother-in-law, Sgt. William Nutley, Royal Wiltshire Yeomanry. Called up 3 September 1939, he was demobbed late in 1945 without ever having home leave.

May and Bill in Cambridge after demobilization.

III

THE PEOPLE

Chapter 1

LEADERS OF MARLBOROUGH

"The highest of distinction is service to others."
King George VI May 12th 1937

I do not believe any book about Marlborough would be complete without an account of some of the contributions made by the leading citizens of the town, especially since the turn of the century. Many became mayors and served the town with honour and distinction, giving tirelessly of their time and money. Perhaps they are the truly famous men of Marlborough. There can be no better way to recreate and understand the town's past than to examine the contributions such men made to Marlborough's business, culture, government and progressive improvement in the quality of life for its citizens. It must be borne in mind that the people of whom I write were for the most part names to me or known by sight only, but I remember hearing my parents talk of them with respect and admiration, and I saw them over the years at town functions. Much of my information has been gleaned from reading and hearing people talk of them, but again it must be remembered that the Atlantic and great lapses of time have lain between me and the town, for except for a few months at the end of the war, Marlborough has not been my home since I was eighteen.

Marlborough was first granted a royal charter by King John in 1204, and though the provisions of that charter were changed and amended several times subsequently, the mayor and corporation up until very recently held considerable power, making the borough almost a self-contained community. In 1815 Marlborough was incorporated into the parliamentary constituency of Devizes, resulting in some loss of power for the town's governing body, but it was within the last decade that local government was completely reorganized and as a result Marlborough now no longer governs itself but is part of the Kennet Area, the council of which makes all governmental decisions. Thus the ancient offices of Mayor and council are now largely ceremonial, their real authority much reduced. In his book *A History of Marlborough* J.E. Chandler lists an almost unbroken line of mayors from 1310 on and the names make interesting reading. A William Bigges (my maiden name though spelled without the 'e' and I doubt there's any connection) served in 1615 and again in 1622 and the old Marlborough name of 'Gough' is seen first in 1722. A Merriman, the first of several, was mayor in 1814 and a Russell in 1831. As we move into more recent times, more familiar names are to be found.

Looking back over the last century or so, it can be seen that certain families stand out as having produced men who served as mayor multiple times. I refer of course to the merchant dynasties of the Frees, the Ducks, the Crosbys, the Harraways among others. Such families were headed by excellent business men who brought their commercial expertise and acuity to running the town, knowing full well that a well run town would mean better business for them and that the resulting prosperity would work to the advantage of both borough and individual establishments. Certain college masters became mayors too strengthening the link between town and gown and adding a cultural dimension to town life. Other mayors were drawn from the professions of law, medicine and government service.

Certain of these men deserve more than a passing mention and perhaps chief among these is Thomas Free. Born in 1850, he was the founder of the furniture firm of Thos. Free & Sons and was mayor on six occasions. He received the O.B.E. for services to the community and at the time of the coronation of George VI in 1937 was acclaimed in the national press as being the only man in the nation to have been mayor of his town at the time of three such happy events, the crownings of Edward VII in 1902, George V in 1910 and George VI in 1937. On March 6th 1947 he was made a freeman of the borough of Marlborough. I remember Mr Free at Marlborough Grammar School Prize Days, awarding the books to the successful students, a rather short heavy-set man with a grey walrus moustache, extolling the virtues of hard work in the strong West Country accent he was proud to possess.

His son Eric followed in his father's footsteps for he too was mayor of Marlborough six times. It was Mr and Mrs Eric Free who masterminded the cultural exchange between Marlborough, Wiltshire and Marlboro, Massachusetts, visiting that town in 1960 when it celebrated its tercentenary. In Marlborough in 1985 I had the privilege of a short visit with Mr and Mrs Free in their lovely house and garden which is tucked away in one of the lanes off the High Street. We found much to talk about, though not enough time, but I was grateful for the opportunity to speak with members of one of Marlborough's first families. Mrs Free was Edna Scattergood, the daughter of Edward Scattergood, for many years master of Marlborough's workhouse and another public spirited citizen. She made a very pretty and elegant mayoress and was a great help to her husband in his official capacity.

Another prominent name in Marlborough was that of James Duck. He was made a freeman of the town in 1953, in recognition of long service to the borough, including holding the office of mayor three times, terms which were spread over three decades. The first was in 1917, the year of my birth, and the last in 1948 when he had the honour of receiving King George VI and Queen Elizabeth when they visited Marlborough. 'Captain' Jimmie Duck as he was generally known, owned stables and ran a riding school. He operated a dairy which had a big share of the college trade, and also carried on a business of motor coach operation and kept cars for hire. His coach was known as 'Billy Boy' and transported many Marlborough people on outings to the sea and elsewhere. I suspect I rode in it on Sunday School trips to Bournemouth, Weymouth and Weston-super-Mare. He was a thin spare man of middle height with closely cropped iron grey hair and a round face with ruddy cheeks. Generally he was to be seen on horseback, clad in impeccably tailored riding breeches and hacking jacket. He was certainly one of Marlborough's most colourful characters.

As I continue to peruse the list of mayors, I am sadly reminded that the businesses founded by many of them have now passed into oblivion. I see the name W.W. Lucy. My father remembered a printing and bookshop of that name, but when I, as a child, clinging to his hand, went into the dark fascinating interior, it had become W.H. Smith. Mr Lucy was responsible for printing a Marlborough Directory. I am the proud possessor of a much dog-eared copy of the 1931 issue and it has been the source of much valuable information.

Another bookshop in the town was owned by two ladies, Miss Flux and Miss Brooks. Miss Flux was tall and plump with a cloud of dark hair, much given to frilly dresses and large flowery hats, while Miss Brooks was short, stocky, bespectacled, always clad in no-nonsense tweed suits, sensible shoes and Henry Heath hats. My father used to buy second-hand books from these two booksellers, particularly those pertaining to local history. Some of these were among the books I brought with me to America and they have proved a rich treasure trove of information.

I see the names Milburn, Colbran and Morrison on the list, the first two ironmongers in the High Street, the latter a member of the family which owned the rope factory in the Parade. Housed in one of the oldest buildings in the town, it was in continuous operation as a rope factory for 250 years until it closed in 1965. Mr Milburn was a partner in the ironmonger's shop known as Milburn and Phillips. In addition to tools and hardware they carried a very nice line of china. I remember a Miss Phillips well. On my first return to Marlborough in 1954 she helped me select a Royal Doulton coffee service and tea set which I bought with money given to me by an aunt. They are among my most cherished possessions. When I came back to Marlborough the next time Milburn and Phillips was gone, their shop occupied by strangers. Mr Colbran was a partner in Dale's, another ironmonger in the town. In fact ironmongers seem to have been good material for the office of mayor for Thomas Pope held it in 1926.

Other tradespeople who served at least one term in the last century were Glass, Jackson, Crosby, Russell, Head, Webber, Burchell, Hillier, Harraway, Cooper, Calvert and Chandler. Mr Glass was a tobacconist on the lower side of the High Street. He had a pretty daughter named Joy. Jackson, Harraway and Calvert were drapers and haberdashers. Russell and Head were tailors and outfitters catering mainly to the college trade, Hillier was a builder and contractor, Burchell a grocer, Cooper and Webber butchers and fishmongers, while Crosby was for many years racquets instructor at the College and senior partner in the sports shop known as Crosby and Lawrence. This establishment in the shadow of St. Peter's Church, supplied most of sports and athletic clothing and equipment required by the College boys. Mr Crosby was mayor of Marl-borough three times. David Chandler, son of Jess, Marlborough's historian, was mayor in 1971. He is associated with the saddlery business which has been continuously operated by the Chandler family for many generations.

Another business man who was mayor in 1893 was Thomas Lavington of the auctioneering firm of Lavington & Hooper. This was the firm my father worked for for many years, though Mr Lavington was dead by the time he commenced his employment there. Mr Lavington was highly regarded in his profession. He had a daughter who became a nurse and eventually matron of Savernake Hospital. She ran the hospital for many years with authority and distinction and under her administration it became a model for cottage hospitals. She was a distinguished figure in her stiffly starched dark blue uniform with snowy white apron and frilled white cap tied primly under the chin, though she walked tentatively as if her feet hurt her. Nevertheless she patrolled the corridors and the wards of the hospital tirelessly, getting to know her nurses and her patients intimately, but visiting her wrath on those who did not measure up to her exacting standards. Though I saw her only on rare occasions she seemed to me the personification of Florence Nightingale.

Another mayor who had a connection with Lavington & Hooper was H.M. Friend, for her was the firm's chief clerk. He and his wife lived in George Lane and the youngest of their five children was about my age and we played together off and on for years. Her name was Margaret but she was commonly known as Babs. She was a lot of fun and full of mischief and had a beautiful head of chestnut hair which I admired and envied. She was quite young when she married a farmer and had several children. The other Friend children were all successful and pursued interesting careers. The oldest, Joy, got a B.A. from Bristol University and taught French until she married and went abroad. Don went to India in a business capacity. He used to appear periodically on long leaves in Marlborough, something I thought quite romantic. Betty became a nurse and later married Mr Kitchen who was the borough surveyor, while Frank emigrated to Australia. Three of the family had very blond hair the colour of ripe corn, while Joy had dark red brown hair like Babs.

Mayors Bambridge, Leaf, Savery, Christopher Hughes, Kempson and Seamer were all college masters, their interest in and successful administrations binding the town and the prestigious public school more closely together. Mr Leaf who was mayor in 1906 retained his interest in the town all his long life. I remember him as an old man of great dignity, heavily built, white-haired and florid of face. When he died his will disclosed that he had left his beautiful Georgian House in Silverless Street facing the Green to the town and it has since made an elegant home for the town council offices. Mr and Mrs Savery lived in a lovely house called Welland which they built at the top of Stone Bridge Lane, the house now occupied by Dr and Mrs Dick Maurice. Christopher Hughes was often to be seen striding around the town with dogs in tow, a strong athletic looking man. He taught art at the college and was a noted artist himself. He was especially known for his etchings of local scenes and many Marlburians are the proud owners of his work. I own several of his etchings myself, some given me by Marlborough friends as wedding presents. Mr Kempson is without doubt Marlborough's best known and definitive historian. His knowledge of the town and its environs is phenomenal and it speaks eloquently of his love for the little town where he has lived for so many years. One of the most interesting men to hold the office of mayor in 1893 and again in 1908 was William Samuel Bambridge who was Director of Music at Marlborough College from 1864–1911. He was a brilliant pianist and organist and was a leader in many aspects of town life, especially sporting activities. He was a New Zealander by birth and when he built two houses in Marlborough he named them after places in his native land, the Waimate in Pewsey Road and Purewa in London Road. The Waimate was quite a landmark in my childhood but for some reason it was demolished several years ago. Howard Lansley was another mayor who was long associated with Marlborough College in a business capacity. Educated at Marlborough Grammar School, where he was an outstanding athlete he has served the town and college well and faithfully in many capacities. He married the former Betty Yeomans, a petite blond beauty who worked in one of the town's fashionable dress shops. She was raised by her mother who was widowed in the Great War.

The mayoral list also contains the names of professional people, lawyers, doctors and governmental officials. The Merriman family gave many lawyers to the town and one had a distinguished career as agent to the Marquess of Ailesbury. Four Merrimans became mayors, serving nine terms beginning in 1814 and spanning three generations. One Mr Merriman, a solicitor and Clerk of the Peace in the town though he never aspired to be mayor, lived in an imposing house called Sempringham off the Salisbury Road. He owned the property on which stood the derelict building which had once housed St. Margaret's Monastery. It was demolished in 1925, but prior to that was a source of much curiosity, ghostly fears and fantasies to me when I was young. Mr Merriman had named his house after the founder of the monastic order, St. Gilbert of Sempringham, a small place in Lincolnshire whence the monk had come. I remember Mr Merriman's daughter, a middle-aged spinster when I was a little girl. She was a large lady with a plain but pleasant face, generally to be seen, dressed in servicable tweeds and shapeless felt hat, in all weathers pedalling her bicycle as she went around doing innumerable good deeds in the town. She would always dismount from her bicycle and take time to chat with us, and while I admired and sought to emulate her upper-class accents I always thought she talked as if she had a plum in her mouth. She was greatly loved by the poor and sick people she visited. They properly called her Miss Merriman to her face, but behind her back called her affectionately if irreverently 'Daisy'. It was years before I saw her name in print and discovered it was 'Desiree'. I thought 'Daisy' suited her better.

Just as the legal profession was represented on the mayoral list by many Merrimans so the medical profession provided many Maurices. This distinguished Manton and Marlborough has given public spirited citizens in many fields to the community for many years but chiefly they have served as doctors. Dr Thelwall Maurice founded in 1792 the family practice which still persists and created a veritable dynasty of doctors. He was the Grammar School doctor and spent much of his time patching up injuries which the boys acquired under the brutal rule of Dr. Lawes. Dr. James Blake Maurice served as a governor of the Grammar School from 1880–1909. He led the town in health improvements and was instrumental in the installation of a good water supply and a system of sanitation. He also established the Iron Hospital to deal with a typhoid epidemic. It was later replaced by an isolation hospital. He also set up a regular nursing service. So many Maurices became doctors in the town that they became known by their Christian names to avoid confusion. Drs. Oliver, Godfrey, Walter, Jim, Tim and Dick have practiced in Marlborough and Drs. Nick and David still do. Some of these found time to serve the town in civic ways too and one, Dr. T.K. Maurice was elected an Honorary Freeman of the Borough on April 24th 1972.

The Maurices also gave Marlborough its first lady mayor. Mrs Cecily Maurice served in 1954. In 1962 and again in 1965 Miss M.E.N. Pearce was Mayor. A daughter of an old Marlborough family who ran a plumbing business and kept a china shop in the Green hard by the churchyard, she had become a teacher at St. Mary's School. She taught Standard V preparing girls for the 11+ exam – I was among her pupils – but when Miss Brunton retired she became headmistress, serving with great distinction in that position. I am sure she ran the town as efficiently as she did her school. Three other ladies followed in Miss Pearce's footsteps as mayor – Mrs Harral who was matron of the Children's Convalescent Home on the Common, Mrs Pocock wife of a prosperous local farmer and Mrs L. Ross.

Much of the work of the mayor and Town Council goes on in the Town Hall, which is also used for many public events, dances and other forms of entertainment. The present building, abutting into the High Street at its eastern end was completed in 1902, the third such structure to be built on that site. Originally a High Cross stood there which was built at the end of the 16th century. A Guildhall was completed in 1389 about in the middle of the north side of the High Street and a later one replaced it, but that one was destroyed in the great fire of 1653. The following year the first Town Hall to be built on the present site was completed. In 1792 this building became dangerous because of the weight of its stone slab roof. The Court Room was dark and cramped and the County magistrates found it inconvenient so the town decided to rebuild as they did not wish the Court Sessions, held in Marlborough at Michaelmas according to ancient privilege, to be moved elsewhere. In 1866 the question of inconvenience for the magistrates again arose and extensive alterations and renovations were undertaken, but the refurbished Town Hall was still felt to be inadequate. Plans were set afoot for a completely new building, which would be Marlborough's memorial marking Queen Victoria's Diamond Jubilee in 1897. While the new Hall was under construction the old Grammar School which had temporarily closed, served as the place where town business was conducted and it was outside this building that Edward VII was proclaimed king in 1901. On October 9th 1902 the first meeting of the Town Council took place in the new hall. It had cost considerably more than the original estimate, but it is a handsome building and functions well. There had been some discussion about an alternative site – the Marquess of Ailesbury had offered the Corn Exchange – but it was decided to build on the site of the two previous halls. In view of the volume of traffic, the present location represents some hazard, but hindsight is always better than foresight. To me its mid-street location gives a nice balance to the town and emphasizes Marlborough's most outstanding characteristic – her very wide street – some say the widest in all England.

It was the job of local magistrates and justices of the peace, who were men of some wealth and standing in the community to try petty crimes, but those of a more serious nature were deferred to Devizes Assizes. The crime rate in Marlborough was not high and most court cases dealt with minor infractions of the law, such as parking illegally or failing to conform to lighting regulations for vehicles. Around Fair time, and holidays and when a locally trained racehorse won a big race, charges of drunkeness and disorderly conduct were wont to increase. Robbery cases were few and most amounted only to petty thievery. There was a manslaughter case involving a Marlborough driver which I remember because my parents talked of it a great deal, perhaps because my father too drove a car for a living. I believe the man was eventually acquitted. The only murder in Marlborough that I knew of occurred during the war when two local girls returning one summer evening to their work at Savernake Hospital were raped and murdered by an American soldier. One of the girls was known slightly to me as she had been for a short while a pupil at the Grammar School. The murderer was quickly apprehended and dealt with summarily in the fashion of military justice, but the town was deeply shocked and frightened. Marlborough seemed suddenly very much in the front line.

Chapter 2

NEIGHBOURS OF THE PAST

"Better is a neighbour that is near than a brother far off."
Proverbs XXVII 10

My 1985 visit was a remarkable stimulant to my memory. In the
old familiar places and flushed with the success of my first book of
recollections, I conjured up thoughts of many people who had
touched my life in the early years. Since many of them were our
neighbours, I will start at my old home, the little row house, later
converted into my father's shop at the junction of the London and
Salisbury roads. There were ten houses in the row known as Bridge
Buildings which followed the curve of the London Road as it went
east parting from the Salisbury Road at the bridge across the Kennet.
The strips of garden belonging to the houses sloped down to the
river. The houses had been built and were owned by a man named
Ernest Piper, a prominent local builder and contractor. He used to
collect the rent every Friday. Mother would always have the house
sparkling clean and tidy and May and I were expected to be on our
best behaviour and only speak if spoken to. I remember him as a
rather portly gentleman, very properly dressed in a grey suit with
gold watch chain spread across his expansive stomach. He wore a
broad-brimmed felt hat in winter and a panama in summer. He
always removed his hat as he stepped across the threshold into our
narrow dark little hall. Mother and Father paid rent for many years
and it was not until a few years before the war that they bought the
house – I believe for two hundred pounds – at which time it was
converted into my father's shop which he proudly named Savernake
Forest Woodcraft.

I can remember very clearly most of the people who lived in these
houses, some couples with children who became our first playmates

and some older people either childless or with grown families. We learned to treat all our neighbours with courtesy and respect. My parents were on good but not familiar terms with our neighbours. Living in such close proximity to other people, Mother sought to preserve her privacy. Only on very rare occasions were we invited into our neighbours' houses, or they to ours, and it was not often that our playmates came into our house – playing with them was definitely an outside activity. People prized their independence, and minded their own business, but when there was trouble in a family everyone banded together to do what they could to help and give support. The gardens, which were not fenced, were off limits to us except for our own and most of them were beautifully kept growing both flowers and vegetables. My mother looked after our garden as Father with all his other activities was not a gardener – in fact he disliked gardening intensely and grumbled very much when Mother shamed him into helping her with the heavy digging in the spring. The houses had a narrow strip of garden in the front with a low wall and spiked iron fence and gate. At one time Mother conformed to the horticultural fad of the day and had it planted with red geraniums, yellow calcelaria and blue lobelia, but later she replaced these plants with dark red wallflowers which used to perfume our front rooms. The houses were covered in Virginia creeper which turned a beautiful crimson in autumn. One house in the row had white jasmine festooning the front door which also gave off a heady fragrance.

We lived in the third house in the row, our address 27, London Road. Mr and Mrs Wheeler and their large family lived in the first house, and we did not know them very well, just bidding them good-day whenever we saw them. There were also several children in Number 26 and we played with them off and on for years, particularly with Betty who was about my sister's age. Their name was Lawrence and they were racing people with the fluctuating income common to occupations connected with betting. Mr Lawrence was what was known as a tout in the racing world and when the horses he bet on or recommended to others won there was rejoicing in the household. Sometimes Mrs Lawrence would give Mother a hot tip and Mother would occasionally risk a shilling each way and would be very happy if the horse won. I remember when Mr Lawrence, a big red-faced Yorkshireman, died and the struggle Mrs Lawrence faced to keep the family together and to provide for the younger children. Several of the older girls were grown and independent, but the only son, Billy, had met with an accident while employed in construction and lived as an invalid for several years before his death, which added to the family's difficulties. But Mrs Lawrence bore up cheerfully. One married daughter Ivy lived at home with her husband Reg Brown, head lad at one of the local stables, a position of some responsibility. They had several sons. One of them Colin, grew up to be a very bright promising young man, but died tragically of polio. The oldest son was killed in the war. I met one of Ivy's grandchildren on my last visit to Marlborough, along with Kathleen (Babe), now Mrs McGuire, the youngest of the Lawrence family. Both work in the White Horse Bookshop. I had difficulty recognizing the rosy-cheeked bespectacled child, some years younger than I, in the well-dressed grey-haired lady who introduced herself to me. Mother and Mrs Lawrence were good friends and confidantes. Mrs Lawrence used to tell her troubles to Mother who was a good listener and Mother admired her fortitude and humour and felt she was indeed fortunate by comparison. Most of the family are now dead but 'Babe' told me that Betty, the girl we knew best is well and prosperous.

On the other side of us lived Mr and Mrs Alum, he tall and bespectacled, she short, dark and pretty and of Irish extraction. Her mother, Mrs Ponting, lived with them and I remember her as a small lady with iron-grey hair drawn back tightly in a bun and wearing gold rimmed spectacles, generally known as Granny glasses. She was always dressed in black, a full length dress of a stiff material called bombazine, made with a high collar decorated with jet beads, into which was pinned a cameo brooch. Her costume was, I suppose, a relic of the widow's weeds of Victorian days. Whenever we saw her she had in her arms a tiny Yorkshire terrier peering through the long hair covering its face and yapping furiously at us. Mrs Ponting had a son who worked for the Marlborough Times. He used to visit her quite frequently. He had lost a leg in the war and limped around on an artificial limb. I think he was in pain much of the time, but I remember him as a kind and pleasant gentleman always speaking kindly and joking with us. He was, I think, the first wounded ex-soldier I knew. The Alums had two daughters, Margie and Edna, who were a little younger than we were. They were our constant playmates when we were very young. Mr Alum died when quite a young man, leaving his wife and family to manage on the very small widows' pension of those days. She took in lodgers to supplement her income, and because she was a good housekeeper was able to look after her home and children well. Mother and she were on good terms but were never close friends. Edna and her husband still live in the same house. Margie married many years ago and made her home in Calne and I heard that she had become a recent widow.

Next to Mrs Alum there lived an interesting family named Groves. Mr Groves was a short dark heavyset man who worked as an engineer for the Post Office while Mrs Groves was very lively and fun to be around. She had reddish hair which she wore in a knot on the top of her head and a few stray ends always seemed to have escaped. Mrs Alum and Mrs Groves had a falling out over a matter unknown to us. As far as I know they never spoke again, though continuing to live next door to each other for the rest of their lives. This made things rather awkward for us as we were on good terms with both families. Mr and Mrs Groves had three very clever children and they were quite ambitious for them. The whole family was very athletic and excelled in sports. The boys and their father were stars in the local cricket and football teams and Eileen was an excellent hockey and tennis player. Len and Eileen were very dark like their father, but Harold had the reddish hair and blue eyes of his mother. The boys did very well in subsequent careers. Harold became a surveyor but was called up at the beginning of the war, gained a commission and had a distinguished military career, staying in the army after the war was over. He married one of Marlborough's most beautiful girls Maureen Cannon, who had the red hair and green eyes of her Irish heritage.

The Cannons were an interesting family, who had spent much time in India since Mr Cannon was retired from the Indian Army. I do not know why they chose to settle in Marlborough, but they were neighbours of the Garsides through whom we got to know them. It was Mrs Cannon who was very much the dominant partner in the marriage. Short, plump, red-haired and Irish she like Maureen must have been very pretty in her youth. She got to know everyone very quickly in Marlborough, had a penchant for gossip and began to serve as midwife, nurse, helper and adviser to anyone who needed such services. She was extremely ambitious marriage wise for her two daughters Madeline and Maureen, the latter appearing to be very much her favourite. Madeline married and Army sergeant, some years before the war and our family was invited to the small gathering after the ceremony at the Cannon's house. The service itself was Catholic and we did not attend and I am not sure where it was held since at that time there was no Roman Catholic church in Marlborough. I well remember the party at the house. There was plenty of good food and drink, and we gathered for singing around the piano. It was the first time I was included in the circle of friends to which my sister and Maureen both belonged. I was not much younger but still at school whereas the others had been working at a variety of jobs for some years. I remember they were surprised and rather chagrined that I received a lot of attention from a very attractive and eligible young man. It developed into my first romance, though it was very short-lived.

After a prolonged period of attempted matchmaking on the part of Mrs Cannon between Maureen and a young master at the Grammar School, Maureen finally married Harold who had been in love with her for a long while. They had one daughter who was also beautiful and red-haired and very talented musically. But after her birth and after Harold went into the army they drifted apart and were eventually divorced. Maureen returned to Marlborough to live with her widowed mother and died some years later in a tragic accident.

It was Eileen Groves who was my closest friend in the neighbourhood. She was a year behind me in school. She had won a scholarship to the Grammar School. She was a very good student and excelled athletically and became a very fine pianist. When she left school she worked for a time in W.H. Smith's bookshop, but soon went into teaching, beginning as an uncertificated teacher, but eventually gaining sufficient credentials to qualify as a head teacher, serving in that capacity in several Wiltshire villages for many years. She also taught music and became very interested in politics. She was active in the National Union of Teachers and was a strong supporter of the Labour Party. Her private life was a sad one. The young man she had expected to marry broke the engagement and married another girl. Shortly afterwards he was killed as he returned from a bombing raid over Germany. Eileen's heart was broken and she never seemed the same again. After her father died she continued to live with her mother until she succumbed to a devastating illness in her early fifties. I saw her when I returned to England and we corresponded sporadically. I grieved for her – she had shown so much promise and had reaped few rewards, though many Wiltshire children must have benefitted from her tutelage. The last time I saw her she gave me a small blue leather bound book of Keats' sonnets. We had read them together when we were at school.

The houses beyond the Groves' seemed to change hands rather frequently. The Garsides began their married life in Bridge Buildings, but moved several times. I remember a postman named Dixon and his family and a railway worker named Pike. His pretty blonde wife was always cleaning and polishing and life could not have been very comfortable for him and their daughter Doris, a ginger-haired rather aggressive little girl. One of the houses was occupied by the Bodman family and he was a signalman on the railway. An elderly couple named Thomas lived in another of the houses. They were childless. He was a gardener and we used to see him striding to work with spade and fork over his shoulder. I was rather afraid of Mrs Thomas. She was a Miss Harraway before she married, was taller than her husband, had a stately figure and moved with great dignity reminding me of Queen Mary. It was incongruous and something of a shock to see her go out on wooding expeditions in Savernake Forest, wearing old clothes, one of her husband's cloth caps put on back to front, pulling a little cart for the firewood she found. I never said more than a timid good-day to her, never went in to her house and was quiet as a mouse when she stopped to talk to my mother. Another old lady I was rather afraid of was Mrs Eden. No child ever dared go near her garden. She let rooms and they were once rented by a couple named Ireland with whom we became very close friends. The last house in the row belonged to Mr and Mrs Duck. He was a house painter, a genial gray-haired man who had a handcart which he used to pull around with all his equipment. We were all saddened when he died unexpectedly after a short illness. Mrs Duck was a fine gardener and I can still see and smell the pinks, mignonette and thrift she liked to grow. She lived to be a very great age, retaining her wit and wisdom to the end. I would generally stop in to see her whenever I was in Marlborough. The Ducks had two children, a daughter who before her marriage worked in one of the shoe shops in the town and a son George who worked in the Co-operative Stores and was married to a pretty Marlborough girl. During the war George was captured by the Japanese in Singapore. It was many months before his wife and mother heard from him, but after enduring all kinds of hardships in prison camps he was set free at the end of the war and returned home to continue his work in the grocery business. I had the pleasure of meeting him in the Green on V-E Day 1985.

The houses in Bridge Buildings are still there. Most have been modernized and the two small living rooms made into one large one. I believe a chiropodist now lives where we did for so many years, treating his patients in what used to be my father's shop. Apart from Humphrey Stone who still lives in one of the houses and Mr and Mrs Piper Cooke who live where the Ducks used to, and Edna and her husband, they are now occupied by people who are strangers to me.

We also got to know other residents of the London and Salisbury Roads and George Lane. People walked a great deal in those days.

Women going on daily shopping errands and people working in the town would walk to and fro, greeting us and, if they had time, stop to talk, so that in course of time we became acquainted with quite a lot of people. Most were superficial acquaintances, but some became friends as common interests were discovered. As my sister and I went to school we walked and played with children nearby. Two of my best friends at St. Mary's School were Peggy Rossiter and Rosie Dobson. Peggy was the youngest of a rather large family, a very pretty child with regular features and light brown hair cut in bangs. She married rather late in life and lives in the house in Bridge Buildings where Mr and Mrs Duck used to live. She loves to walk and is often to be seen on the downs, in the forest or meadows. She is still beautiful. Rosie – her name was Rosina and some people called her Ina – had strawberry blond hair cut in a bob and tied on top with a big bow. Her eyes were blue and she had many freckles. I played a lot with both these girls and loved them very much, but lost touch with them after I went to the Grammar School. I also liked the two Hatchman girls, Vera and Iris. Their father was a policeman and they lived in the Police houses in George Lane. Iris married an American during the war and now lives in Vermont. A family named Cook lived across the road from us and their two girls, Queenie and Winnie, were good friends too. Queenie was a tall delicate stoop-shouldered girl and Winnie was very pretty with dark hair cut in fringes so that she looked to me like a Japanese doll. I believe she lives in Pewsey now.

On the other side of London Road were two rather nice semi-detached houses which belonged to an elderly lady named Mrs Gardiner. She lived in the smaller of the two along with her daughter Mrs Aylen and her two sons Cyril and Monty Aylen. Monty was in the same class as I in school. He was full of fun and mischief but died an early death from lung cancer, Cyril spent most of his life in Marlborough and was a popular member of the community. The Gale family lived in the other house. Mr Gale owned a printing business in town and his brother A.W. Gale was a nationally known beekeeper. There were four children, but the only one I knew at all well was Diana. She had the most beautiful red gold hair, and was very studious and bookish. She became a librarian. The houses were covered in ivy and creeper and in the garden of one, on the corner of the London and Salisbury Roads was a huge red horsechestnut tree, covered in spring with pink candle like blossoms and in autumn was a source of the shiny conkers we liked to play with.

A little beyond our house and on the opposite side of the London Road was a dairy farm belonging to Mr and Mrs Purdue. They owned about a dozen cows and we would meet the animals a couple of times a day going out to pasture and back to be milked. The Purdues had a milk round and people used to leave their pint or quart jugs outside to be filled from milk cans. Mr Purdue was a well set up man always dressed in breeches and leggings while Mrs Purdue was plump and apple cheeked. She always wore a coat type overall and a wide-brimmed hat. They had several children but tragedy struck the family when Mrs Purdue died still a young woman. Years later one of the boys was to lose his life in the war. The farm and adjoining cottages are gone now and replaced by more modern housing. Although my mother knew and liked Mr and Mrs Purdue, we did not get our milk from them but from Mr Sinden who also lived in the London Road. He and his wife had one daughter Vera, who was a friend of my sister. Mr Sinden served us for many years. He brought the milk in a horse and cart, ladling it out from big churns into the jugs my mother left out. No one seemed to consider it an unsanitary method of milk distribution. When the weather was hot and thundery Mother used to bring the milk to a boil, believing this would prevent it souring, for we had no refrigeration.

There were two small grocery stores in our neighbourhood. These little shops were to be found in every part of town, often on a street corner and they sold sweets, tobacco products and a general line of groceries to people living nearby. There was one on the corner of Salisbury Road and George Lane, and we patronized it a good deal. It changed hands frequently and we always seemed to be on very good terms with the proprietors. The other one was kept by a couple named Pond, and I was sent on frequent errands there. It is now the London Road Post Office. I doubt that the owners of these small shops made much of a living, but they seemed to like what they were doing and served a useful purpose in the neighbourhood and were places where friends could meet and exchange news and gossip. Many tradespeople in my childhood days employed errand boys or delivery men, so there were many callers with whom my mother could exchange greetings and pleasantries. I think these people were important in her rather lonely life and she regarded some of them as good friends.

Marlborough's London Road ran from the Grammar School on up a steep hill to Savernake Hospital and the edge of the forest. At the town end the road forked three ways one leading through Barn Street and the Green and Herd Street to the Common, the others, New Street and the Parade led to the High Street. There were several stores and business establishments in the Parade and New Street and

London Road, though they were smaller and less prestigious than the High Street shops. A couple named Holland kept a nice sweet shop on the corner of London Road and Barn Street. Mrs Neate had a greengrocer's shop – she was a small talkative lady and one of our favourite people when we were children. There was another green-grocer in the Parade whose name was Hillier. Mother thought he grew the best tomatoes and one or other of us was sent frequently all summer long for ½lb of them. They were hothouse grown, small and rather orange in colour, very different from the crimson giants our garden produces today, but they were very good and we all enjoyed them.

Today Chandler's saddlery shop occupies the corner premises where the sweet shop used to be, but at the time I was growing up it was in a different location in London Road. The shop sold riding equipment and leather goods, many of them handmade and also housed a Branch Post Office, a great convenience for dwellers in the eastern part of town. Somewhere around 1930 a young lady came to work at the Post Office. Dark-haired and pretty, her name was Rose Ferguson. Jess Chandler, son of the saddler, fell in love with her and married her. Ro's father, a native of Scotland had been a keeper working for the Marquess of Ailesbury. He was called up to fight in World War I and lost his life in the ill-fated Gallipoli campaign. Her youngest brother, Andrew, who was a classmate of mine at the Grammar School, was born after his father's death. By the grace of the Marquess, the family continued to live in the Lodge at Leigh Hill and Ro talks of the way her mother worked to provide for the six children, all of whom turned out to have successful satisfying lives. Ro and Jess were close friends of my sister May and her husband Bill Nutley. They were friends indeed during my sister's long illness and when May and Bill died within a few months of each other, the Chandlers stood in loco parentis to their two daughters.

Jess Chandler died in July 1985. He was one of Marlborough's best known citizens, doing much to document the town's long history. He was born in Marlborough in 1911 and was educated at Marlborough Grammar School where he was a contemporary and friend of William Golding. When he left school he joined his father in the family firm of saddlers which had operated in Marlborough since it had been started by an ancestor in 1796. Possessed of many talents, he was a fine piano player, playing principally by ear and was much in demand at local functions and dances. In fact my earliest memory of Jess is his returning to Marlborough Grammar School – he had left the school as I entered it – to play for the three "Set" socials which were held annually in the old school dining room. Jess went to Canada to try his fortune there but returned to the saddlery shop to join his father in the business. He remained in Marlborough for the rest of his life except for six years of war service. He joined the Somerset Light Infantry and Gold Coast Regiment and this took him to Africa. During the war we often used to see Ro, who at that time lived in George Lane, walking with their two little tow-headed boys, David and Chris. A daughter Rosemarie was born to them after the war. Always much interested in local history and archaeology he began writing on subjects dear to his heart many years ago. He began in 1951 with *The Postal History of the Gold Coast*, then in 1965 published *A History of Saddlery*. He continued with his very popular *A History of Marlborough* in 1977, following it up with *Marlborough – Local Place Names* in 1980. His boyhood interest in the mutiny on the Bounty developed into a deep study of the subject, which resulted in three books – *Beloved, Respected, Lamented* (1973), *This is Mutiny, Mr. Christian, Mutiny* (1975), and *In the Shadow of the Bounty* (1977), and international recognition as one of the definitive authorities on the subject. Jess was in many ways the epitome of the complete Englishman – craftsman, tradesman, writer, gardener, golfer, sailor, traveller, raconteur, a fiercely loyal citizen of his town and county. He was a slight spare man of middle height, with sharp features and humourous eyes, his speech with its slow West Country burr proclaiming the Wiltshire roots of which he was so proud. He was a good husband, father and friend to many. He knew the satisfaction of a long and happy marriage, of success in his craft and avocations, of seeing his children grow up and embark on interesting careers and happy family lives. His older son David, a Cambridge graduate, now heads the saddlery business. Public spirited he has served on the Town Council and in 1971 was Mayor of Marlborough. Chris is an oil engineer in Houston, Texas and Rosemarie, married to Christopher Loveday is raising a young family in Marlborough. We last saw Jess in May 1985. Happy in the new little house they had built in the orchard of the home they had occupied for many years and where Rosemarie now lives, he looked thin and frail. His mind however was keen as ever, his sense of humour unchanged, his love of Marlborough still very much apparent. He talked of a visit he had had recently from a wealthy American executive who had come to him for imformation about the Bounty and he laughed at the incongruity of their hired Rolls Royce parked in the narrow lane leading to their house. Jess Chandler was our friend and my mentor. We will sorely miss him.

There was a public house in the London Road with an interesting sign – The Five Alls. As a child I used to look at the five panelled sign and speculate on the illustrated captions –

> The King – I rule all
> The soldier – I fight for all
> The lawyer – I plead for all
> The bishop – I pray for all
> John Bull – I pay for all.

Perhaps John Bull was Everyman and the original picture of him at the Marlborough inn was thought to be a portrait of the first landlord. I have learned that the Alls signs came from Holland and are to be found mainly in Wiltshire and Gloucestershire. Sometimes there are Four Alls, sometimes Five, sometimes Six. The Devil – I take all – is the sixth. The earliest instance of the sign is thought to be the one at Marlborough. Interestingly enough, a young man named Timothy Williams, a present resident of Chapel Hill was brought up in the Five Alls.

There was another pub in London Road, at the place where Elcot Lane goes off to the left. It was the Roebuck, though commonly known as the Buck. A family named Cope kept it years ago and we knew their three children, Clara, Georgie and Beryl. On my last visit to Marlborough we had a meal there in an attractive modern lounge bar, very different from the dark little poky place of old.

There were several rather nice large houses in London Road, often standing cheek by jowl with more modest homes. One of these – I suppose it was really in Barn Street – was called Wye House and was a fine Georgian residence which belonged to a gentleman with the impressive name of Herbert Vavasour Langdale Kelham. He was the mayor in 1930 and I remember him as a tall aristocratic looking man, grey-haired and mustachioed, clad in impeccable tweeds and always accompanied by his faithful collie. He used to visit my father and the two would enjoy long conversations. He gave the land to the town on which the war memorial is constructed. When he died the house was first turned into flats, then became a boarding annex for the Grammar School, now I believe it is made into flats again. The house is surrounded by beautiful grounds and is shaded in front by one of the most spectacular copper beech trees I have ever seen. Next to Chandler's establishment there was ivy covered Moffat House, belonging to a man named Smith who ran a drapery business. The name Moffat came from Scottish antecedents and when Mr Smith retired he built a bungalow further up London Road which he called

Wee Moffat. Mayfield was a big red brick Victorian house just beyond where we lived. It was shielded from the road by a wall and a line of thick tall evergreen trees. It is now replaced by a block of flats. The house belonged to a family named Hugill. Several brothers and sisters, middle aged to elderly when I was a child, lived together. The youngest, Miss Rose, ran a private school for young children and girls and some of the students from the Grammar School boarded there if transportation to and from their home villages was not available. It was considered quite the "in" thing to board at Mayfield and those who did so were quite a snobbish clique – at least they had that reputation. The boarding of Grammar School students always presented a problem for the school authorities. At one time some were boarded in the homes of townspeople. When I was very small, so that I can barely remember them, Mother had two girls, farmers' daughters from near Enford. Their names were Poppet and Etta, unusual names for those days, but they only spent one term with us, transferring to Mayfield when it became available. The Hugills were well-educated, gentle people, the ladies small and birdlike and the men, also small, generally appeared deep in thought. One habitually walked with his hands clasped behind his back, head sunk in abstraction. They were all musical and often could be seen toting 'cello or violin. Across the road from Mayfield was another large house, a comparatively modern one called Combe End. It belonged to a Miss Curtis who lived there with a companion and a beautiful white Samoyede dog with long silky hair. She employed a chauffeur named Perryman who lived in Salisbury Road. My mother was a friend of Mrs Perryman. They had one son Edward who was about my age. Combe End is now a home for senior citizens. Axholme was another large house owned by an elderly childless couple named Redman. It has now been converted into office buildings.

The residents of our immediate area seem to me now to have been very interesting people and I wish I knew more about them, whence they came and what ultimately happened to them. I can recall their faces and appearances as clearly today in my mind's eye as I saw them then. A Methodist minister lived a few doors from us. His name was Champion and he suffered from facial cancer and wore a false nose in consequence. This upset me very much and I was terrified that I might acquire a similar illness. He was always cheerful and ready to talk and Mother held him in high regard. When he was moved in accordance with his church's ministerial policy he was replaced by another very charming man.

Though Mother was proud of her Church of England affiliation and I believe in consequence felt somewhat superior to her "chapel" acquaintances, she had a great liking and respect for the Wesleyan and Congregational ministers she knew. Well educated, true Christian men, many of them were drawn from families of the labouring or lower middle classes and consequently could understand and identify with the problems of their congregations. In this they contrasted with many Church of England clergymen who were often aristocratic by birth and generally public school and Oxford or Cambridge educated. Though many of them were dedicated Christian leaders of their flocks, church livings were held by some as sinecures and awarded by preference. Some churches were well-endowed and gathered tithes from rich farmlands, and the rector or vicar, especially if he came from a wealthy family was sometimes able to live the pleasant life of a country squire, paying minimal attention to his pastoral duties. Others were able to pursue intellectual or cultural interests. Some were the younger sons of landed gentry who were unable to share in the family land by the law of primogeniture. Such young men turned to the army, navy, law, medicine or the church for a career. Those in the church did not always live up to Chaucer's ideal of the parish priest –

> God's law and his apostles twelve
> He taught, but first he followed it himself.

Some found it difficult to understand the problems of the poor simply because they came from a different class. Some made a name for themselves in literature or scientific pursuits, at the same time performing their priestly roles in exemplary fashion. George Herbert, who was the Rector of Bemerton near Salisbury, though not a Wiltshireman by birth was the perfect parish priest as well as the author of some of the finest religious poetry ever written. Robert Herrick was also another West Country poet and parson, and Gilbert White of Selborne in Hampshire was a naturalist who documented animal and plant life in his village during his long tenure there as rector, deeply loved and revered by his parishioners.

Marlborough was generally fortunate in the men who were the rectors and curates of the town churches. Canon Wordsworth who lived before my time and was rector of St Peter's from 1897–1911, was a distinguished ecclesiastical scholar and local historian, and was much loved by his people and still talked of in my memory. The first rector I remember was Canon Host. He was an elderly gentleman

with a florid complexion, always dressed in black with clerical collar
and shovel hat. He used to visit the infants' and girls' schools to teach
us the Catechism and I thought for a while, presumably in view of
his name, that he was the personification of the Holy Ghost. He was,
I think highly respected and well liked, but never seemed to get
really close to the people. He was followed by Canon Jones, who
prepared me for confirmation and the Church of England examination in Religious Knowledge that entrance to Whitelands College
required. He was a good, kind man, but rather narrow-minded and
fundamentalist in his views and beliefs. Canon Swann married us.
Aristocratic, autocratic, intellectual, good in the pulpit, tall, thin and
hawk-nosed, he left me with the feeling that he was not very
understanding of human problems.

Returning to London Road, there was a pretty little stone and flint
cottage just beyond our house which was occupied by a rather
eccentric old lady, but eventually became the home of the charming
Gardiner family. Mr. Gardiner was a jockey and had a beautiful
blond wife, a lovely daughter Joan and two red headed boys. Joan
was married to a British officer a few days before our wedding. An
old lady named Miss May lived in a house called Rosslyn. She was
tiny and prim but nice to talk to. Miss Pierce was an English teacher
at the Grammar School and she had built a pretty little house in
London Road called Wychwood. Mother and I were occasionally
invited to take tea with her. She was very small, with a little round
applecheeked face and she wore granny glasses that were always
slipping down her nose. Perhaps these spectacles gave her the
sobriquet she had at school – that of Granny. She taught literature
and I credit her for the knowledge and love of it I have to this day.
She was very religious and especially interested in African missions
and in a leper hospital supported by the church. She used to sell
lace-trimmed handkerchiefs, modesty vests and other small articles
made by the patients. After she retired she gave most of her time to
church and charity work. She lived to be a very great age. London
Road seemed a favourite place for teachers to live. Mr Barcham, the
headmaster of St Peter's Boys' School lived there with his wife, the
former Sally Pope and their three daughters, Margaret, Barbara and
Pauline. Margaret and Barbara were about my age but Pauline was
many years younger. Our parents were good friends and Margaret
and I liked each other a great deal. I always admired her rose petal
complexion. Mr Barcham was a very highly respected teacher, a
strict disciplinarian who expected a lot from, and got a lot out of his
boys. I worked for him for several months before leaving for

America. He influenced generations of Marlborough's boys and is still remembered by many today. Mr Pontefract, the headmaster of the Grammar School for many years, lived with his wife in a nice house on the corner of Stone Bridge Lane called Greenlands. After he retired the man who replaced him, Mr Stedman, lived in Greenlands with his wife and five children. Marlborough Grammar School grew and developed rapidly under Mr Stedman's leadership and he was also the author of several text books on religion, *A History of Marlborough Grammar School* and a very complete erudite book on local history entitled *Marlborough and the Upper Kennet Country*. Approaching retirement age, but hoping to see the school move into the new building on Granham Hill, he suffered a severe stroke and died after living for several years in Aldbourne. He is well remembered by his former students, myself among them. It was a great pleasure in 1985 to receive a telephone call from Pam, one of Mr Stedman's daughters.

Mr Sawyer, another teacher at St Peter's School also lived in a bungalow in London Road. A widower with a small son Geoffrey he married a Miss Harraway. In addition to regular teaching he also taught woodwork and subjects which today would be called industrial arts. As a woodworker he had much in common with my father. We used to see him, a small frail man cycling to school in all weathers. A family named Heath used to stop and talk quite often. Mr Heath was a gardener and their cottage garden was a wonderful sight all spring and summer. They had a son and two daughters. The older daughter was courted for years by an older gentleman named Mr. Large. However whenever we saw them they were always accompanied by Mary's younger sister Vera. I wonder if they ever married, and if so, if Vera lived with them.

I suppose the people I have written about were fairly typical of any small market town in the south of England at the time I was growing up. But it seems we had many characters and I would like to know what happened to them in the succeeding years and why they were the way they were. The lives of many of the older people were dominated by custom and convention and in the case of the poorer people by "knowing one's place". But most of these people while seemingly satisfied with their own lives wanted something more for their children. At the time I was growing up we were still a class-ridden society, everyone getting along well but with certain very clear demarcations. Aristocrats were by turns autocratic, benevolent, paternalistic, patronizing, concerned, condescending. Professional people were much the same. There was a growing independence in the middle class as they made their way up and then there were the poor, burdened with large families, quietly accepting of the social order and most of them too concerned with obtaining the basic necessities of life to be otherwise, though a few young ones were always ready to break away if the opportunity should arise. Stirrings of socialistic thought were slow to come to a town like Marlborough, yet there were the faint beginnings of change and questions were being raised in the minds of some. The Great War and the sacrifices of the common man, better education and the decline in the fortunes of the privileged classes began the process and World War II gave it a great impetus. While in general Marlborough has remained loyal to the Conservatives, in common with the rest of the country it has enjoyed the many improvements brought about by socialist legislation. Today class distinctions are blurred but not entirely eradicated. Laws can guarantee civil rights, better living conditions and educational opportunities, but there still remains a gulf between the haves and the have-nots, the ones who have the benefit of centuries of privilege behind them and those who have only their innate abilities.

Chapter 3

OLD FRIENDS

"Should auld acquaintances be forgot . . ."
Robert Burns.

My mother's obituary notice in the *Marlborough Times* in April 1946 contained the phrase that she was of a retiring disposition. It was very true – she liked staying home, keeping her house in order and her eye on her two young daughters and she was always home when my father came in from his erratic work schedule and his own habit of working and talking to friends without much regard for time. The phrase should not be taken to mean that she had no friends for she had many acquaintances and a few very close lifetime friends. I have written at length about some of these people in my previous book or in other parts of this narrative, but there are others who deserve more than a passing mention, for they played some part in our lives and added colour and interest to what without them would have been a rather drab existence.

Mr and Mrs Garside were our parents' closest friends and I am glad that I have kept in touch with their three sons, Philip, Alan and David, the first two now retired from insurance and banking careers and David head of the auctioneering firm that his father took over from Lavington and Hooper. Mr and Mrs Harvery, he, head cashier at Lloyd's Bank were also good friends and Mr and Mrs Ireland brought their story of romance and adventure to our limited experience. A couple I have not mentioned previously were Mr and Mrs Lang. They lived in George Lane and he held a position of some responsibility in the Post Office. He was a very handsome man with strongly marked features and an air of asceticism, while his wife was plump and comfortable looking. He was strongly religious, a churchwarden for many years, and he and my father were prone to discuss religion, with Mr Lang always hoping to convert my father.

The Langs had a son and a daughter, grown when we were children. Mary inherited her father's good looks and also his religious convictions for she became a missionary and eventually married one. We exchanged many Sunday teas with this couple and always enjoyed going to their house and having them visit us. Sunday tea was the popular time for entertaining and the hostess would go to considerable trouble to provide a wide variety of bread and cake.

Mother always liked to get to know our teachers, especially when we went to St Mary's School and some of them came to tea quite often. Miss Brunton was the headteacher of St Mary's when we first went there and Mother liked her and respected her. She was a fine example of the dedicated high principled women who gave the best of their very considerable intellect and talent to their pupils. She was the only teacher who ever caned me – for being late for school. My dignity I believe hurting more than my hand, I received no sympathy from my mother, who pointed out that she had sent me out in plenty of time and therefore the responsibility was mine. I have rarely been late for anything in my life and wonder if Miss Brunton can be credited for the punctuality which I consider one of my virtues. When Miss Brunton retired she went to her house in Lainey's Close looking forward to years of leisure, but she developed intestinal cancer and died after a lingering illness. Our first teacher in the infants' school and later our music teacher was Miss Collins and she and my mother were very close friends until she too died of cancer. In Standard I we had a teacher who was thirtyish, plain, with straight dark bobbed hair and pince-nez glasses. She was not one of our favourite teachers but she and mother got along well, so she visited us often. She came from a remote village in the south western corner of the county and lodged in Blowhorn Street with an old lady who was very deaf. Her life indeed seemed bleak and she accepted Mother's invitations with alacrity. Imagine our shocked surprise when she failed to turn up in the classroom one Monday morning and news leaked out that she had eloped with a man unknown to all but her landlady who judged him to be an unsavoury character. We never heard from her again. Mother was very chagrined and never discussed the matter with the two of us, and we knew better than to ask questions.

A young teacher who brought a ray of sunshine into our lives was a Miss Nurding, who I believe came from Trowbridge. She was an ebullient young girl, just out of college, with rosy cheeks and rimless glasses. She taught my sister in Standard II. She was engaged to be married and we enjoyed hearing all about her wedding plans. My most vivid memory of her was seeing her come to Mother in tears just before Christmas because she had lost her handbag which contained the month's salary she had just received. Though I was only about 6 at the time I can still recall the tragic poignancy of her loss. When she left to be married – marriage in those days meant giving up a teaching job – she gave us a book called *Everyday Stories to Tell to Children*, and it was a favourite for many years.

Mr and Mrs Fullager were another couple with whom my parents were friendly. I remember going to a lovely Christmas party at their house once at which a trifle thick with whipped cream was served. I was disappointed in it because the sherry it contained was too strong for my childish taste. This couple had three daughters, the youngest of whom, Joy, died of meningitis when she was about eleven. These warm friendly outgoing people seemed to change and grow old overnight and though I was only a child myself I dimly realized what the loss of a beloved child can mean.

Mr Fullager was the manager of Sloper's, a general clothing store in Kingsbury Street just around the corner from the High Street. The parent company was in Devizes and the branch in Marlborough was thriving, being the premier store of its kind in Marlborough with a bigger volume of trade than the family business of Harraway and Say. Mother got most of our clothing from Sloper's, underwear for the two of us, lingerie and corsets for herself and heavy wool underwear for my father. She also bought his shirts, generally of flannel in a striped pattern. They were collarless, the collars being bought separately, white and heavily starched, fastened to the shirt with studs. My Mother spent a lot of time starching and ironing these collars until they were stiff and shiny. When the time came for me to go to the Grammar School we got my school uniform at Sloper's and she also bought material by the yard when she decided to have most of our dresses made by Miss Hutchins, a dressmaker who lived in a lane off London Road. When we were children we always looked forward to a visit to Sloper's, especially if we were able to mount the green carpeted stairs at the back of the shop to the first floor, where all ladies' clothing and intimate apparel was sold. The shop had a surprisingly large inventory of clothing and all kinds and sizes and everything from hats to stockings, from underwear to outerwear could be found there though the choice was sometimes limited.

Mr Fullager was always to be found in the men's department and he had a capable assistant in Humphrey Stone, a dark handsome young man, one of our neighbours and a faithful and ardent admirer of my sister for many years. He spent the war years in India but came back to Marlborough to work in Sloper's until it closed. After May had worked at Savernake Hospital for a few months and decided nursing was not the career for her, Mother approached Mr. Fullager about an opening in the shop for her. When one came up, May began to work there, continuing for several years until she transferred to Boots, when a branch of that pharmaceutical chain opened in Marlborough. The life of a shop assistant was quite hard, involving long hours of standing and very little time off. There were certain advantages, such as meeting people, some buying privileges and getting first choice as things came into the shop. May was a pretty girl with shining brown hair and large hazel eyes and she looked most attractive in the black or navy blue dresses that the salesgirls were required to wear. She was well spoken and had good taste so that she was able to advise customers positively yet tactfully. Though the pay was low, she liked the work and made many friends both with her fellow workers and her customers. Saturdays were always very busy and I remember how tired she used to be and how she complained of her feet, but she generally recovered in time to go out to the "pictures" or a dance and she never lacked for escorts. Wednesday was the highspot of the week for her for it was early closing day for the town businesses. She finished at 1p.m. and always had something interesting planned for that afternoon and evening. To be an assistant in a nice or high class shop was considered a good job for a girl (or boy) leaving school between the ages of 14 and 16. It was generally, and especially for a girl, a dead-end job with virtually no prospect of advancement, but after a few years most girls got married. There were a few older women who worked in local shops for many years, generally living with their parents. These women came into their own during the war when men and young women were called up. These older ladies were able to use business and managerial skills learned from long experience and during the difficult days of the war they did more than their share to keep things going on the home front.

It was always sad to hear of the death of a child and it happened more frequently than it does today as present treatments and medicines are so much more effective.

One child I remember who died of cancer was eleven-year old Arthur Marchant. He lived in George Lane with his parents and two older brothers. One was named Peter, a contemporary at Marlborough Grammar School of Jess Chandler and William Golding. He was an outstanding athlete and a rival to Bill both scholastically and athletically. Arthur had just entered the Grammar School when the disease struck, appearing first in his leg but soon progressing to more vital parts. We used to see his mother pushing him in a Bath chair. The handsome little boy, pallid from his illness, was always dressed in his grey school uniform, proudly wearing his maroon school cap with its castle crest and 1550 date. He died, I recall, on August 9th which is my birthday.

Were we as children preoccupied with disease and death as they came to members of our community? Certainly we heard our parents talk of it, though cancer was a hush-hush subject and nothing was ever told us of the facts of life. Babies either came in the doctor's black bag or were deposited in some unexplained way by the stork. Illness of all kinds was dreaded by our parents, largely because death could follow a quite ordinary sickness. 'Flu – and everyone remembered the terrible world wide epidemic that came at the end of the Great War – or a cold often turned to pneumonia, and many children succumbed to whooping cough, dipheria or scarlet fever. T.B. was common and generally fatal – it's only treatment a belief in fresh air and good nutrition, the former easier to provide than the latter, but neither a cure, only a prolongation of doomed life. Death was discussed openly in our home and in our religious classes at school, in the sentimental fashion of the day and most of us when young believed that death meant going to Heaven or resting safe in the arms of Jesus. I think I worried more about losing my mother or my father than dying myself.

What in many ways seemed even sadder than a death was to see a family burdened with a retarded or handicapped child. When it occurred, the parents seemed to accept it with resignation, if not with equanimity, and most women – the burden fell largely on the mother – devoted a great deal of time, energy and love to the care of such a child. As time passed the greatest worry seemed to be over the fate of the child when the mother died or grew too old to care for it. We used to see one girl very often, always with her mother. We were told she suffered from St Vitus's Dance, but I think today it would be called cerebral palsy. Another couple we knew had a Mongoloid daughter. I will never forget the shocked tone of my mother after seeing the baby for the first time, telling my father later, "That baby's not right". Such tragedies were common enough in small communities such as Marlborough and seeing them must have impressed me deeply for I can remember them clearly, though none concerned us intimately.

A middle-aged couple named Draper were rarely seen without Mrs Draper's brother Percy Farmer. He was a cripple lying helplessly with leather bound stumps of legs and in addition suffered from a nervous disorder which affected his speech and caused jerky uncontrolled movements. They pushed him in a special cart with sides of basket and he was always clean, well-dressed and groomed and obviously surrounded with loving care and affection. The trio was always accompanied by a black and white terrier of mixed ancestry, led on a leash by Mr Draper while Mrs Draper pushed her brother. I think the Drapers kept a small sweet shop in the Parade, though my memory is not quite clear on this point. What deeply impressed me as a child so that the remembrance of them has stayed with me is the filial devotion expressed in a lifetime of care for a helpless man. The Drapers were ordinary people living a life of heroic sacrifice and service which in the passage of time became the very reason for their being. Perhaps such people are the true heroes of places such as Marlborough.

Another of Mother's friends was Mrs Dance. She lived to be 100, outliving most of her friends and contemporaries. As I remember her she was tall and spare, with iron grey hair, of indeterminate age, an emphatic way of speaking and an air of competence and authority. She had had two sons, sadly one a lifelong invalid and the other killed in the 1914 war. This young man left a pretty fiancee named Frances who after the war married a man named Harry Razey. Mrs Dance had by this time acquired a pretty little house in the Parade just as it entered Kennet Place, and she offered a home to Frances and Harry, looking upon them as her children. When a little girl Mary was born they were all overjoyed. We sometimes visited them for tea and Mary and I were good friends. She was an excellent student at the Grammar School and married a man from Swindon where she still makes her home. For many years Mrs Dance helped care for sick and dying people and was very much a presence in the town. It was sad that both the Razeys predeceased her and her last years were marred by illness and loss of faculties.

Death was accepted with sorrow, but with resignation and I think, a better realization then, than now, that it is inevitable and as natural an occurrence as birth. Among the poor it often created great economic hardship. A widow collected 10 shillings a week government pension with a small additional allowance for each dependent child. Few poor people had much insurance. Sometimes the churches, fraternal organizations or charity helped out and employers sometimes made small contributions, but women in such circumstances had to find some way to supplement their income. Sometimes if their houses were suitable they took in lodgers, but often the only work available to them was housework or laundry. "Charring" was not only hard, it was menial and poorly paid and looked down on, while the difficulties of taking in washing in the damp English climate without mechanical appliances can only be imagined. A widower with a young family was in no better circumstances for he had to find housekeeping and child care help. After a decent interval he generally married again – there were many women left single by the depredations of the first war and often such ladies were glad to find a husband and did a fine job raising motherless children. Women rarely married again. Eligible men were few and far between and any who were available were reluctant to take on an existing family. If either of my parents had died young I do not know how the one left would have coped and I know that such an eventuality was deeply dreaded by my mother.

When a person died it was more often in the home than in a hospital. Bodies remained in the house for several days before being taken to the church for the burial service and internment. This created a difficult period for the family. When a funeral procession passed, the coffin often on a hand drawn bier, all the houses along the way drew their blinds as a mark of respect for the dead, and people made an effort to stay off the street at that time so that prying eyes would not intrude on the family's grief. There were older women in the town who went in to "lay out" the body and prepare it for burial. Such women served several useful purposes among the poorer elements of the town. They often acted as midwives and perhaps occasionally operated as back street abortionists. Certainly they were known to prescribe herbal concoctions, often fortified with warm gin, for girls and women who found themselves in such unfortunate circumstances, though results were by no means guaranteed. I have since thought that these were able women with considerable management skills, locked by poverty in circumstances from which there was no escape. Their ability to cope and provide necessary but often unpleasant services was backed up with comfort, consolation and good advice. Maybe in earlier times they might have been considered witches.

Though illegitimacy was not exactly common, such births occurred from time to time, along with the preferable alternative of a hasty marriage. Both happenings were dreaded by the parents of girls, more I think, because of the disgrace than the added cost and disruption of life resulting from another mouth to feed. Once the child was born it was generally accepted as a family member, receiving its share of love and attention though the stigma of bastardy lingered on. Among the very poor, children were often neglected, ill-fed and ill-clothed, but the neglect arose from ignorance and shortage of funds rather than lack of love or sheer cruelty. In contrast some poor parents went to great lengths of self sacrifice to give their children chances that they had been denied. My sister and I were among the fortunate few who had thoughtful well intentioned parents who went to great pains to provide us with good nutrition and medical care and many opportunites for intellectual and cultural growth, in spite of their very limited funds. Most of our friends came from similar homes.

It was early in the thirties that my father fell in love with beekeeping – a love affair which was to last the rest of his long life. Beekeeping brought us into contact with many people, some of whom became good friends. In his capacity as Local Bee Expert, for which he was paid a small fee by the Wilts County Council, he visited many villages for talks and demonstrations. As a beekeeper he was greatly influenced by Mr Larry Pearson of Vernham Dean. This was a picture perfect village on the Wiltshire/Hampshire border, and for a time our whole family made many Sunday afternoon visits there, going there via the motor bicycle and side car which Dad purchased for his beekeeping expeditions. I wrote at length of the Pearsons in my previous book, and I remember them fondly as people who opened up for me a whole new dimension in the art of gracious living.

My father had been introduced to beekeeping by Mr Shewry and for quite a while Mr and Mrs Shewry and their youngest daughter Margery were fairly constant visitors with the two men discussing bees. Mr Shewry was a tall angular man with an iron gray moustache and a prominent Adam's apple accentuated by the wing collars he habitually wore. His wife was plump, white haired and rosy cheeked, his daughter pretty and blond. When I saw her in 1985 – she is now Mrs Kerrison – she looked exactly as I remember her mother.

Two bachelor brothers, Tom and Victor Chun, sometimes used to visit us. They were both very musical – Victor was a church organist and Tom, who had been a cook in the Royal Navy was a good pianist. When we got our piano we used to have a lot of fun with them. Once I remember Tom iced our Christmas cakes doing a very professional job. They had twin sisters who were ladies' maids to two wealthy women who travelled a good deal and spent a lot of time in the Far East. They were caught there along with their employers and interned by the Japanese for the duration of the war. Another rather regular visitor for some years was the Reverend

Stacey, curate of Marlborough. He was highly intellectual and very well read but rather ineffectual as a preacher and clergyman. He had a wife who was mentally unstable and whose behaviour was erratic and difficult. He seemed to like visiting us and we were sorry when he left to take up the living of Easterton near Devizes.

Mother also welcomed any friends that May and I brought to the house. When May worked at the hospital we got to know many nurses who would stop in for tea on their days off. Later her colleagues from Slopers and Boots would visit. Likewise my school friends Molly Trollope and Gwyn Burgess were always welcome and a strong attachment developed between Gwyn and my mother.

One young friend of my parents was a classmate of mine in school whose name was Walter Reynolds though he was known to everybody as Bunny. One day he summoned up courage to speak to me in school – boys even in the same class did not speak to the girls unless there was some attraction. There was none in this case and in fact he was much interested in a pretty blond girl named Denise Smith who came from Aldbourne and boarded at Mayfield. He asked me if he could stop in at my father's workshop which was at that time in Brown's Buildings in Salisbury Road. He said he had heard Dad's lathe running and badly wanted to see what he was doing. I spoke to my father and in due course Bunny stopped in to see him. A strong friendship grew between this boy and Dad. In fact Dad I think began to regard him as the son he had never had and I must admit to experiencing a few pangs of jealousy as hitherto I had been very much the apple of my father's eye.

Bunny came from a remote outpost of Burbage called Ram Alley. His mother was a war widow and he was her only child. She was badly crippled by arthritis, always wearing high black boots and only walking with the greatest difficulty. They lived in a tiny cottage and existed on her small government pension. Bunny had won a scholarship to Marlborough Grammar School and received an additional grant from the county. He used to cycle to school, making the twelve mile round trip every day in all weathers. He was a good student, being especially good in maths and all the sciences. He was outstanding in practical subjects such as wood and metal work. For rather more than two years, this boy would go from school to my father's workshop where he would spend a couple of hours helping Dad and learning from him some of the intricates of wood turning, carving, marquetry and cabinet making. A wonderful working relationship grew up between them, my father enjoying teaching such an apt pupil. He always came home to tea before setting off on the long cycle ride through the forest and though my mother really welcomed him, she used to complain to me that he was eating her out of house and home. He was a tall raw-boned youth with the insatiable appetite of adolescence and my mother's good food was, I feel sure, far superior to that to which he was accustomed.

When he left school he joined the R.A.F.. He discussed his future plans with my father and Dad felt that one of the services would present a good opportunity for a boy with such a practical bent. Enlistments were being encouraged with the war drawing near. He had by this time got over his infatuation with Denise and met and married another girl a little later on. He became a rear gunner in the air force and was killed early on in the war in a bombing raid over Germany. His death hit us all very hard, especially my father. His poor mother, who had now lost her son as well as her husband in war, never did recover from the shock, becoming quite deranged and finally I think had to enter an institution.

In the hectic years before and during the war, many sudden friendships developed with so many people here today and gone tomorrow. Evacuees from London and other danger areas came into Marlborough and of course servicemen, mostly British at first, but later on they seemed to come from the four corners of the world. By that time I had completed college and had begun teaching in Birmingham, but my sister was in Marlborough and she had many friends whom she introduced to my parents. My gregarious father liked meeting new people and this was an aspect of the war which pleased him. It also brought him much business for the woodcraft business he had begun just prior to the war. My mother gallantly supplied tea for countless people until the stringent rationing made it impossible.

After the war when my mother died, life changed vastly for my father. No longer was she there to provide tea for his many friends and acquaintances. I was in America, my sister newly married and like everyone else trying to adjust to the difficult conditions of the early days of peace. Many old friends rallied round my father and did what they could to help. The Garsides were among them and two young men, Bunny Baker and Oliver Fowler were good to him. He was however never the same again. He missed her good meals, her tidy comfortable house and most of all her companionship, ability to listen, her common sense and her love.

I feel sure that the greatest pleasure he had in his last lonely years was the 1949 visit he made to America. We were living in an apartment on Long Island at the time and this gave him easy opportunity to explore New York City. We took him to Greensboro, North Carolina, where he met David's family. He gave a talk – about Marlborough – to the men of the Buffalo Presbyterian Church; a church incidentally founded in 1759 by some of my husband's ancestors. During the time he was with us we moved to our first house in Glen Rock, New Jersey and Father was of much practical help installing appliances, building a fence and babysitting two year old David. The American visit provided Dad with material for many talks both formal and informal, his experiences over the years becoming, I am sure, much embroidered by his very vivid imagination.

Chapter 4

FAMOUS MEN

"Let us now Praise Famous men . . ."
Ecclesiasticus XLIV. 1

While Marlborough cannot claim to be the birthplace of any very famous men, the lives of certain important historical figures have touched the town in a variety of ways. Some think the name comes from Merlin, king Arthur's wise man, but he is legendary rather than historical, though the town bears as its motto, "Where now lie the bones of the wise Merlin."

Four kings can be said to have had a strong connection with Marlborough. Henry II, the first of the Plantagenet line, granted Marlborough quite early in his reign to his youngest son John. John enjoyed the hunting in Savernake Forest and married his first wife, Isobel of Gloucester in the castle at Marlborough. When the marriage proved childless he divorced her on grounds of consanguity. When he became king in 1204 he spent a lot of time in Marlborough with his second wife and several of his children were said to have been baptized in the old black marble font which stands today in Preshute Church. His son Henry III was frequently in Marlborough after he inherited the throne and he celebrated Christmas 1219 with great festivities in the castle and also held his mother's funeral feast there. He farmed the land and bred stock at Barton Farm and in 1267 held a parliament in Marlborough which enacted the Statutes of Marlborough, in which the rights of the small landowners were set down just as Magna Carta in his father's day had indicated the rights of the barons. The great castle was abandoned after the Wars of the Roses, but passed to the Seymours of Wolfhall in the reign of Henry VIII when he married his third wife Jane. Their son, the boy king Edward VI gave money to the town for the foundation of Marlborough Grammar School in 1550, after which Marlborough's royal connections appeared to lapse.

On March 10th 1498, Thomas Wolsey of Norwich Diocese and son of an Ipswich butcher, exercised his right of choice to receive holy orders in any church of his preference, and so the future cardinal was ordained priest by the Suffragan Bishop of Salisbury in the church of St Peter and St Paul in Marlborough. Wolsey rose to the high office of chancellor in Henry VIII's reign, but had fallen from favour and died before the king married Jane Seymour in 1536.

Sir Robert Cecil, first minister to James I died in Marlborough on May 24th 1612. The actual place where he died is unclear, for some say his death occurred in the Marlborough parsonage, others say it was in the monastery of St Margaret. He was taken ill while travelling from Bath to Hatfield. His chaplain left an account of his death scene, "Though sinking rapidly he insisted on standing erect while prayers were offered, and then gripping his priest's hand died peacefully without a struggle". His body was embalmed and taken to Hatfield for burial.

Oliver Cromwell was in Marlborough during the Civil War, for the town changed hands several times and the fighting was fierce. Cromwell stayed at the George Inn and the story goes that the Marlborough blacksmith nearby refused to shoe his horse, rather surprising in view of the fact that most of the townspeople were supporters of the Parliament. Cromwell must have had some kind feelings towards Marlborough for when the 1653 fire devastated the town he ordered a collection to be made and the money used for restoration and repair. Within a year St Mary's Church was rebuilt.

Marlborough was mentioned in the writings of the three great diarists of the 17th century, John Evelyn, Samuel Pepys and Celia Fiennes. Charles II had visited the town in 1663 and a few years before, Evelyn had been to Marlborough which he described as "lately fired and now new built". Pepys visited in 1668 and wrote – "Before night come to Marlborough and lay at the Hart, a good house and a pretty fair town for a street or two; and what is most singular is the houses on one side having their pent houses supported with pillars which makes it a good walk." The White Hart is no longer there, its place in the High Street occupied by Prout's Cafe and Duck's Shop. Most of the penthouse has been preserved but part of it has unfortunately been removed, for it is one of the town's most famous features. Celia Fiennes who rode about England on horseback recording her impressions in the reign of William III was most impressed by the house in the process of being built which is now "C" House of Marlborough College. She wandered about the grounds noting the bowling green, the clipped hedges, the fish-ponds and the Kennet. She climbed the mound and noted the tumbledown building atop it. She admired the view from Granham Hill "with its two church towers and its very large streets and the Kennet turning many mills."

In the next generation the Seymour House achieved some social and cultural fame in keeping with the fashion of the day. Lady Hertford, who was born a Thynne of Longleat became an ardent admirer of pastoral Wiltshire and especially of her Marlborough home. She wrote many letters praising the house and became the patron of several men of letters and poets chief among them Stephen Duck, thresher of Charlton, in Wiltshire, a bucolic poet of little merit and James Thomson, a Scotsman of some genius but little success. He is chiefly noted for a long four-part poem called *The Seasons*, the type of pastoral verse particularly pleasing to his patroness and part of which he most certainly wrote in Marl-borough. But both Duck and Thomson eventually proved disap-pointing to Lady Hertford who in her later years suffered great sorrow at the death of her only son and lived to see her mansion that she had loved so well turned into the Castle Inn by the daughter who had inherited it.

Dr Sacheverell, notorious rather than famous was born in St Peter's Rectory in 1674, and received his education at the Grammar School. The Hancock brothers, Thomas and Walter, born in 1786 and 1799 respectively were sons of James Hancock, timber merchant and cabinet maker of Marlborough. Thomas was the founder of the India rubber industry, while Walter adapted steam locomotion for road use. John Hughes, a minor poet and playwright was born in Marlborough in 1677. He was the author of a successful tragedy *The Siege of Damascus*, but his other work was marked by mediocrity. William Golding while not a native of Marlborough spent his boyhood in the town and received his education at the Grammar School.

By 1760 the Seymour mansion had become a hostelry, the Castle Inn. As a very fine lodging house on the main road between London and Bath, which had become a very popular spa and watering place under the leadership of Beau Nash, it attracted a high class clientele. Its most famous visitor was without a doubt William Pitt, the Earl of Chatham who in 1767 returning from Bath suffered a painful attack of gout. He shut himself in his room at the Castle Inn and we are told "his domestics occupied the whole inn and wore the appearance of a little court". In 1813 there was a collision between two coaches three miles from Marlborough and a well known architect, James Wyatt was killed. His body was taken to the Castle Inn. The Duke of Wellington was forced to take refuge in the inn on the night of December 26 1836 because of a snowstorm. Impatient to get to his destination which was Badminton, he set out next day but his coach and six horses had to be dug out of the drifts at Kennet. Many travellers chose to stay at the Castle Inn rather than face bad weather, darkness or highwaymen in the wild downland country that lay west of Marlborough.

Jess Chandler.

David Chandler, Mayor of
Marlborough 1971–72.

Outside St. Mary's Church after our wedding on 15 March 1944.

A civilian once more. David in Central Park, New York, January 1946, a month before my arrival in the States.

Mayor James Duck escorts
King George VI and Queen
Elizabeth from the Town
Hall, 19 March 1948.

My father standing by a fallen oak in Savernake forest, about 1950.

Parenthood. David aged 4, Christopher aged 1, 1951.

Family life.

Retirement.

Selling *Recollections of a G.I. War Bride* in Ridgewood, New Jersey.

V–E Day ceremonies at Rambury's War Memorial. A group of Marlborough men are in the foreground

V-E Day memorial service at Marlborough. Philip Garside, President of Marlborough's British Legion lays a wreath at 11 a.m.

The author today.

IV

THE WARS

Chapter 1

WAR AND WAR AGAIN

> "And blood in torrents pours
> In vain – always in vain
> For war breeds war again."
> John Davidson

Most of us who were the war babies of the Great War spent our childhood very much in the shadow of its aftermath. I was more fortunate than many of my contemporaries for our family life was not disrupted by the war and we suffered no personal loss. Yet fear of unemployment kept my father locked in a poorly paid job as unrewarding in intellectual stimulation as it was in monetary compensation. While young women bereft of their husbands and fiancees provided a source of excellent teachers our poor school buildings and lack of all but the most basic equipment were due to an economy almost bankrupted by the war.

Looking back on those years between the wars, the twenties and thirties, it seems that Marlborough in common with the rest of the country survived the depression years, reached a short period of relative prosperity and then came late and reluctantly to the realization that another war loomed ahead. As children of those years, my contemporaries and I heard a lot about the Great War, much talk of men lost to us, hushed whispers of those wounded and disabled, admiration for those decorated for gallantry, sympathy for widows and orphans. We participated gravely and with varying degrees of understanding in solemn ceremonies of remembrance. Armistice Day, with its symbols of white crosses and red poppies and with services with all the sad panoply that the British can muster so effectively and dramatically, impressed us deeply. A lump always came into my throat and my eyes hurt during the two minutes silence beginning at the stroke of 11 on November 11th and I always dreaded I would sneeze, cough or otherwise disgrace myself during that time which seemed interminable. We read World War I poetry – the idealism of Rupert Brooke and the realism of Siegfried Sassoon admiring both. My father became an enthusiastic member of Toc-H, a mystical organization formed in the trenches and continued in peacetime to help ex-servicemen and promote international understanding. Many of our friends belonged to the British Legion, an organization which throve in Marlborough as elsewhere. But we also heard our parents talk of low pensions and raw deals for men who had given their all for their country. As the depression worsened we realised that there were parts of the country far worse off than Marlborough which by comparison was a safe little town making a living off agriculture and the education of the rich and privileged. Mostly though for us they were happy years, made so largely by loving and understanding parents.

For a few years in the late twenties and early thirties we seemed to enjoy a period of relative peacetime prosperity but it was not long before disturbing currents of war talk were apparent. By 1930 such talk was being given some credence, though the proponents of it were generally dismissed as prophets of gloom and doom and most people refused to consider seriously the prospect of another war. My father was one of the few to harp on another war theme so subconsciously I was more aware of the danger than most young people my age. By the time I was fourteen we were seeing a lot in the papers about Hitler in Germany and Mussolini in Italy. Hitler's emphasis on youth and its organization, its ideal of Teutonic racial purity, in those days, I'm afraid, rather appealed to us. We read of the horrors of the Spanish Civil War, the nightmare of Abyssinia, but fully believed the cup would pass us by. The Reichstag fire in 1933 upset us briefly, but starting with the Sudetenland we went from crisis to crisis only momentarily disturbed by each. Yet a few desultory preparations for war were taking place, though we were either largely unaware of them or considered them quite unnecessary. Young men were being encouraged to enter the armed services either as a full time career or on the Territorial basis. Many flying schools were opened, mechanization of the army proceeded apace, air raid shelters were built in high risk areas. A civil force of wardens, fire fighters and auxiliary police was trained and many factories switched from their peacetime manufacture to the making of armaments and tools of war. Even so Britain and her allies were off to a slow start and by 1937 it dawned on most of us that we were hideously unprepared to take on Germany's armed might. We greeted Chamberlain as a life-saving hero when he returned from Munich in 1938 declaring Hitler had missed the bus. A few months later it became obvious that it was the prime minister who had made the gravest miscalculation. When Hitler attacked Poland, as had been his intention all along, we could make no further concessions, had to fulfill our treaty obligations and face another war. The only good thing about the shameful Munich pact was that it bought us a year of precious time.

Most people who had lived through the 1914 war envisaged that the second war would be fought in the same way, in the trenches of Northern France the opposing armies contesting bitterly for every inch of blood-soaked soil. But added this time would be the danger on the home front of air raids and gas attacks, so that all of Britain and her people would be essentially in the front line. No longer could the country shelter behind the narrow strip of water that had hitherto so effectively defended her in the past from the attacks of continental armies. And yet in the final analysis once the brave pilots in the Battle of Britain had turned back the Luftwaffe's onslaughts it was England's insular position that kept the German armies from invading. The trenches though were a thing of the past. This time it was global war and in 1939 all British forces that could be mustered were sent to the Middle East, India, Hong Kong or Singapore, leaving only a few regiments for home defense and the formation of a small British Expeditionary Force which was sent to France.

For the next five years the war dominated and directed our lives. Conscription went into effect immediately and all able-bodied men under 35 were eventually called to the colours. Only the most cogent reasons of health and the most essential of occupations could keep them out of the armed forces. Women too were called up to man the home front, work in the factories and on the farms. Many girls served in the women's services – the A.T.S., W.R.N.S., and W.A.A.F. – freeing men for fighting duty. As a teacher I was in a highly reserved occupation and our war duty lay in organizing the evacuation of school children and doing double duty to cover for the men who were called to fight. "Carry on" became our watchword. Our daily lives were governed and controlled by food rationing, clothing coupons, travel restrictions, inconveniences too trivial and many to mention, blackouts, air raid precautions, assigned spare time duties such as fire watching, our lives played out against the ever present danger of air attack and invasion. Willy-nilly everyone was totally absorbed in the war effort. The backdrop to our lives were our personal worries for sons, husbands, lovers, friends at the front and the ever changing news which came to us via the newspapers and the wireless. The 9 o'clock news bulletin became an institution in many British homes. Every Sunday night it was preceded by the playing of the national anthems of our allies until they became so numerous that the practice had to be discontinued. For a long time it seemed the news was always bad, but lightened here and there by the indomitable spirit and sense of humour always displayed by the British when they have their backs to the wall. The rallying points in those dark hours were the fighting speeches of Winston Churchill who succeeded the ailing Neville Chamberlain as prime minister in May 1940 when we appeared completely crushed by the fall of France.

But the small British army struggled back from Dunkirk and regrouped, the Home Guard was formed, the tiny Spitfires and Hurricanes turned back the German Messerschmidts, our cities withstood vicious air attacks, convoys of food and arms continued to evade the U-boats and reach us from across the Atlantic. The treacherous attacks by Japan, while robbing us of Singapore and Malaya and imperiling Australia and New Zealand also brought the Americans in. In fact the attack on Pearl Harbour was greeted in Britain with something of a sigh of relief – "Now the Americans will have to come in." I remember saying just that over Sunday tea in Birmingham. And come they did in their thousands and with their massive military might to save the world for the second time in a generation.

Although young people bear the brunt of service and sacrifice in a war yet war is easier on them than on older people. Those years were the times that try men's souls, yet we glimpsed what Wordsworth meant when he wrote of the French Revolution:

> Bliss was it at that dawn to be alive
> But to be young was very heaven.

It is ironical yet true that in the midst of war's horrors, man can reach great heights of courage, self-sacrifice and idealism and we as young people shared briefly in those moments that stood out from the tragedy and weary boredom of the times. We lived in the depths but occasionally knew the heights and the latter compensated in some way for the former. I would not have had it otherwise. The youth of England formed a band of brothers just as men who serve their country in war know a special kind of camaraderie. The war changed the predictable course of our lives, sometimes tragically, but often opening up avenues to new life.

Chapter 2

VICTORY 1945

"The German War is therefore at an end."
Churchill broadcasting on V-E Day May 8th 1945

"Let us join in thanking Almighty God that war has ended throughout the world and that in every country men may now turn their industry, skill and science to repairing its frightful devastation . . ."
King George VI V-J Day August 15th 1945

As V-E Day 1985 approached I tried to cast my mind back forty years to the day that brought the end of the war in Europe, but to my chagrin I had no clear memory of how I spent the day or how Marlborough celebrated it. I was probably too concerned that it did not mean the end of the war, too worried about what might be in store for my husband and anxious also about my mother's persistent ill-health. I was living in Marlborough, teaching at St Peter's School, it was on a Monday and we had a holiday from school. I do remember the church bells ringing their message of victory out loud and clear – bells silenced since the fall of France in 1940, only to be rung in the dread event of German parachutists falling from the sky.

By the war's end Marlborough had suffered the loss of 37 of her young men. The sadness at each was felt throughout the town for the smallness of the place meant that each was known to the other. Others were to come home wounded in body and spirit, many after long periods of incarceration as prisoners of war and none were to be again the carefree happy youths who had left.

Though people in Marlborough had been as slow as the rest of the country to recognise the inevitability of war, the years prior to 1939 had brought some prosperity and unusual activity to the rather sleepy little town, as the army and flight training schools nearby were rapidly expanded. The town was filled at weekends with recruits and their visiting families looking for food and lodging which the town strove to provide. This state of affairs continued well into the war until shortages and stringent rationing cut short the economic boom. When the Americans came in force in 1942 and 1943 they brought more money than their British, colonial and European counterparts and in spite of the difficulties Marlborough tried to cater to their needs. The public houses in particular throve. They became the meeting places for conversation and camaraderie and were filled to capacity even when beer and food ran short.

While I was not living in Marlborough during the first years of the war, I made brief visits home from heavily bombed Birmingham where I was teaching or from remote villages to which I was periodically evacuated along with children from that city. I came to the conclusion that country towns such as Marlborough seemed to thrive during the war more than the big cities, which suffered from actual or threatened air-raids, or small villages which remained in isolation, often made worse by petrol shortages and curtailed bus and rail service. In the small safe towns servicemen congregated, made local friends, were entertained publicly and privately and life went on at a heightened pace, in spite of wartime aggravations of blackout, shortages and the terrible winters of 1939 and 1940. The fear after the fall of France in 1940 was offset by local involvement in the Home Guard, pride in the R.A.F. and simply "carrying on", and as the weeks went by there was rising optimism that the danger of German invasion had passed.

Marlborough's position on the main London–Bristol road brought a lot of military traffic through the town and the easy parking in the High Street meant that it became a stopping place. Prior to D-Day, Marlborough became extremely busy, for she was on the main route to the invasion areas, yet not close enough to the coast to be sealed off or evacuated. Marlborough was fortunate too in her evacuees, for she played host to boys from the prestigious City of London School, which shared the educational facilities of Marlborough College.

We had known victory was coming ever since the success of the D-Day landings on 6 June 1944 and the general steady advance through France and into Germany in the weeks which followed. But the latter part of 1944 and the early months of 1945 brought setbacks as well as victories, air-raids involving pilotless planes and rockets and the surprisingly strong German counter-offensive which took place at Christmas in the Ardennes and came to be known as the Battle of the Bulge. This was of special concern to me for my husband was "over there". Nevertheless victory was in the air – the only question, "When?"

Between D-Day and V-E Day many of wartime's annoying restrictions were relaxed and life began to assume some degree of normality. Some of the British troops who had been overseas since 1939 were posted to home duty prior to early demobilization. My brother-in-law, Bill Nutley, a Pewsey man, was among them. As a trooper in the Wiltshire Yeomanry, he had been called into active duty on that fateful 3 September 1939. His regiment, complete with horses, was sent to Palestine as part of a cavalry unit, in an attempt to stabilize that volatile part of the world and guard the approach to India. Later, the horses were replaced by tanks and his unit was sent to North Africa to fight under General Montgomery. After serving as a "Desert Rat" in the see-saw conflict between Montgomery and Rommel he took part in the invasion of Italy and fought up the long peninsula in some of the bitterest fighting of the war. He arrived back in England early in 1945 and after a long leave he was posted to Cambridge. He and my sister May were married a month after V-E Day in London and began their married life in Cambridge prior to his release from the army, when they returned to Wiltshire.

London acclaimed the coming of peace with great celebrations. Churches held services of thanksgiving. Churchill made a speech, the King and Queen appeared on the balcony of Buckingham Palace and the young Princesses were allowed to take part in the public festivities. The provincial towns and villages all had their own ways of rejoicing. There were of course those who did not rejoice – those who had lost loved ones or were still waiting for news of those missing in action. For those too who had lost their homes and possessions in air raids, victory had a hollow ring, for life would never be the same again. But the biggest stumbling block to complete involvement in victory celebrations was the inescapable fact that the Japanese war was not over, nor on 8 May 1945 could its end be considered near. My husband, in France on V-E Day and making a victory speech in halting French to the local populace in Bayon in Alsace Lorraine, had written me of plans for transfer to the Pacific theatre of war. It was hard to celebrate victory with such a prospect ahead. But the momentous decision to drop the atom bomb hastened the end of the war in Asia, the Japanese hastily capitulated and United States units slated for Far East duty were turned around to return Stateside for early demobilization. V-J Day came on 15 August. David arrived in Marlborough on leave saying he had seen newspaper placards in Paris announcing "Bombe Atomique". We celebrated the final victory together though with nc sure knowledge of when and where we would meet again.

But in between the two days of victory there was a significant defeat. Churchill, architect of victory, was rejected by the people in the general election held in July and was replaced as Prime Minister by Labours Clement Atlee. The "winds of change" had begun to blow several years before Harold McMillan coined the phrase, and the British Empire was already shrinking in spite of Churchill's avowed intention not to preside at its dissolution. Churchill's great ally from across the Atlantic, President Franklin Delano Roosevelt had died in Warm Springs, Georgia in April 1945 and so it fell to two relatively unknown men, Atlee and Truman to lead the peace. There was no arguing with death and democracy. These were the men who made the momentous decision to drop the atom bomb. Was it right or was it wrong? The argument still goes on. One thing is certain – it brought a speedy end to the war against the Japanese.

But V-E Day and V-J Day, along with victory and the cessation of hostilities brought many problems of adjustment. Family life had to be re-established. Fathers had been away in the armed forces for years, mothers working outside the home in factories and on farms. Many children had been sent to rural areas for safety's sake and some had even gone to the colonies or to the United States. So many houses had been destroyed or damaged in the air raids that the housing shortage was extremely acute and many families who had lived for the day when they would be reunited now found they had nowhere to live. The conversion of an economy geared for war and drained by it, to the needs of peace, was not easy. People grew impatient at continuing shortages and food, fuel and clothing rationing went on and on. Even the weather failed to co-operate, and the bitter winters at the end of the war added to the general misery. Of the returning servicemen, some were wounded in body and mind and all were changed from starry-eyed youths to hard-bitten veterans uncertain of their reception and concerned about their future. The older people who remembered the sad years after World War I were prepared for a long period of disappointment and disillusion, but the returning servicemen and their famililes who had faced years of "carrying on" grew impatient at the continuing restrictions and the very slow process of returning to normality.

For the large number of young women – Marlborough had several – going to the States, Canada and other foreign parts as wives of men they barely knew, the feelings of most vacillated between high elation and cold feet. As long as the war was on, leaving home was somewhere in the future, but now the prospect of going to a new land was much closer and the thought of joining a husband, married in many cases on wartime impulse, was daunting and frightening though at the same time it was devoutly to be wished. But still the women were kept in suspense for many months and it was not until early in 1946 that the U.S. Army put into effect its system of transportation of the brides its men had left behind them. Many mothers and fathers mourned the departure of their daughters as they sent them off to an unknown country and an uncertain future. The young woman found that America too was settling down after the war. The adjustment to peace was less traumatic than for England and Europe but nevertheless very real and it added to the homesickness that most of the girls experienced in the first few years.

But the war was over and on those two days in May and August no fears of the future, no dread of Russia, spoiled the sweet taste of victory. Only a deep sadness remained that it had been dearly bought with the blood of our finest young men and women and the disruption of life for a generation.

Chapter 3

V-E DAY 1985

"Men of splendid hearts . . ."
Rupert Brooke

Forty years have passed since peace was signed with Germany and special services of remembrance were held in every town and village, at every war memorial on May 8th 1985. In Marlborough a short and simple ceremony planned by the British Legion giving thanks for victory in memory of their fallen comrades was held at 11a.m. at the War Memorial. The day was fine, but cloudy and cold with a bitter wind blowing. The service was attended by Legion members and a few bystanders. Oscar Fulk, my husband David and myself were the Americans present, all of us proud to be there. It was planned as a short low-key act of remembrance of the day that forty years ago ended the war in Europe. A similar service would be held on August 15th, V-J Day, but the main ceremony would come as usual on the National Day of Remembrance which is November 11th, or rather on the Sunday which is closest to that day. Philip Garside as president of the Marlborough branch of the British Legion made a short speech, his words lost in the wind and the noise of passing traffic. As he laid the wreath of scarlet poppies at the base of the monument he recited Lawrence Binyon's oft-quoted lines –

> They shall not grow old as we that are left grow old,
> Age shall not weary them nor the years condemn.
> At the going down of the sun and in the morning
> We will remember them.

After a brief prayer and a moment of silence the service was over. We were left each to his own thoughts, to greet each other and to talk of the war and the dead as we studied the names of the 37 Marlborough men who gave their lives in World War II. These names were on a bronze plaque in the centre of the cenotaph. They are flanked by the names of the 105 men who died in World War I. In addition there is a memorial to Marlborough's war dead in the Lady Chapel in St Mary's Church. It comes as a shock to most people, especially Americans, to see how many more men were lost in the 1914 war than in the later one. The figures represent the hideous waste of life that went on in the stalemate in the trench warfare in northern France for four long years, and in the abortive diversion at Gallipoli. They also reflect the advances in medical science which saved many men in World War II who would have faced certain death in the earlier conflict twenty years before. In World War II however the civilian casualties were much higher.

All the legion members and old soldiers were wearing their medals which dangled from the many coloured ribbons denoting the theatres and campaigns in which they had served. Several men were displaying a beautiful gold medal which hung below the others. This was the medal awarded by France to members of the British Expeditionary Force which was sent to France in 1939 and was literally snatched from the jaws of death at Dunkirk in the fateful summer of 1940. Though Churchill said of Dunkirk that wars had not won by evacuations, victory finally rose, like the phoenix from its ashes, from the retreat at Dunkirk and the brilliant sea rescue operation which followed and in which almost every boat owner in the British Isles played a part. Just as in 1914 Britain's "contemptible little army" held the Kaiser, so in 1940 the Dunkirk operation enabled the bulk of the army to return to England, regroup and live to fight another day. One man, Chappie Green wore on one of his ribbons a bronze oak leaf cluster denoting a mention in despatches for particularly meritorious service. John O'Keefe, in addition to his war service ribbons wore the blue-green one of the Falklands war. In his capacity as chief coxswain of the QE II he had helped ferry troops to the far-off theatre of that most recent war.

In the Legion Clubroom after the ceremony the talk, sometimes sad, sometimes light-hearted was all of the war and the inevitable question, "Where were you on V-E Day 1945?" It was surprising to hear so many say that they were on their way to the Far East and knew nothing of the cessation of hostilities until several days later. Even then victory meant little to the men who had another war still to settle. We left the clubhouse thoughtful and rather sad, yet proud to have shared a few moments with British veterans, many of them known to me in the past, on such a special day.

Again I noted the special kind of comradeship that exists between men who have fought in a war that strained every nerve and demanded the utmost. It is a brotherhood that knits them together and transcends class, education, interests, place of origin and station in life. What Shakespeare wrote of the men of Agincourt is just as true of the veterans of World War II –

> We few, we happy few, we band of brothers,
> For he in war who sheds his blood with me
> Shall be my brother.

After a good lunch at the Wellington Arms in Marlborough's High Street near St Peter's Church, David and I drove to Bowood, beautiful house and estate belonging to the Marquess of Lansdowne, though at present occupied by his son and heir, the Earl of Shelburne. It is just outside Calne, another Wiltshire market town about the size of Marlborough. On the way we stopped to take a picture of the Cherhill White Horse framed in a fold of the green downs, the Monument piercing the blue sky on the right, while in the foreground was a field of brillian yellow rape in full bloom bounded by a split rail fence – a lovely sight and a view that I will one day paint. The horse, a fine high stepping beast, was cut by a Calne physician in 1780 and the Lansdowne Column was erected by one of the marquesses to mark the birth of a son to Victoria and Albert, a son who late in life became Edward VII.

The little grey stone town of Calne distresses me as I see the bacon factory belonging to Harris being demolished. For many years it was the chief source of employment in the town and Wiltshire bacon was famous all over the country.

The cold of the morning had given way to sunshine and though the wind was still keen the sun high in the sky had a little warmth to it. We turned off the main road at the entrance of Bowood and drove through the surrounding woods, full of sturdy oaks and silver-trunked beeches, the tops of which were just showing a hint of spring green leaves. We saw many fine pheasants, the cocks particularly colourful in the spring season and learned later that they are bred for the table and can be purchased frozen in the estate shop. There were many clumps of primroses in bloom and a few areas showing a bluish tinge promised a magnificent bluebell show in a few days' time. The green velvet lawns around the house sloped down to a shimmering lake across which we could see the Doric temple typical of the "follies" so beloved by 18th century landscape planners. Its white columns were reflected in the shining waters. As at Tottenham House Lancelot ("Capability") Brown had masterminded the laying out of the grounds. The lawns were dotted with fine trees, among them oaks and sweet chestnuts and several Lebanon cedars of giant size and antiquity. Planted informally in natural settings were hosts of daffodils of all shades of yellow and white, perhaps a little past their best but still spectacular. The house rebuilt in a smaller edition of its original size is an example of pure architectural symmetry and is fronted by a series of terraces with ornamental flower beds. The roses will be magnificent in a few weeks. The rooms open to the public are very fine and because of their smaller size more intimate than those in many great mansions. We saw the library in which Joseph Priestly, encouraged and sponsored by the first marquess, and the librarian at the time, discovered oxygen on August 1, 1774. We visited the lovely chapel, the walls hung with priceless paintings of Biblical scenes and we admired the fine collection of art the family has gathered from the four corners of the world, sculpture and tapestries being displayed in the Orangery which was designed by Robert Adams.

Bowood at one time was the centre of a literary circle. The first marquess 1737–1803 knew and entertained figures such as Samuel Johnson, Oliver Goldsmith, David Hume and Benjamin Franklin. The Washington family was known to him. The third marquess 1780–1863 along with Louisa his wife had wide interests in art, music and literature. They gathered many of the leading writers of the day around them, among them the Irish poet, Thomas Moore, Lord McCaulay and Maria Edgeworth the novelist. Thomas Moore lived in nearby Sloperton Cottage for several years at the invitation of the Lansdownes, and died there in 1852. George Crabbe, another poet was drawn into the Bowood circle.

Upstairs there was a fine display of paintings, some by famous artists such as J.M.W. Turner and many watercolours of Far Eastern scenes by a Major-General Gosset. We saw too the many beautiful objets d'art presented to the fifth marquess who was Viceroy of India 1888–1894. I couldn't help reflecting how at one time not so long ago the aristocratic families of England had dominated and influenced the world in many spheres. And then I thought how appropriate it was that on the 40th anniversary of V-E Day we should visit the home of a family that had helped make England great, to see their way of life, which twice in a lifetime had been saved by the heroic sacrifice of ordinary Englishmen. But the Lansdowne family had made their sacrifices too. The 7th marquess was killed in Italy in 1944, just a few days after his younger brother had died. And in the first World War the 5th marquess lost his younger son at Ypres in 1914.

We were back in Marlborough by 6 o'clock to get ready to go to Ramsbury to attend the community service of Thanksgiving for Victory which was to be held at the church there and had been arranged by the Ramsbury branch of the British Legion. We drove there with Joan and Oscar Fulk and Chappie Green and the ride in the calm of the evening was beautiful in the essentially English way with the light softening and yet delineating whatever was in our view. The way led us through the tiny village of Mildenhall, past the Stitchcombe vineyards – strange to think of Wiltshire wine – through the hamlet of Axford and the green water meadows of the River Kennet, Axford evoking memories of good times at the Red Lion when the Fulks were landlords there. We passed broad fields and homesteads and fine old woods and we caught just a glimpse through stately wrought iron gates of the beautiful Georgian mansion that is Ramsbury Manor. On all sides the blackthorn hedgerows were white with blossom, the ground underneath starred with the enamelled gold of celandines and the pastel yellow of primroses.

Ramsbury is a large village, more like a small town really and it is dominated by its large and ancient church. The present building dates from the 13th century, though there was an Anglo-Saxon church built on the site of which no trace remains, and there is a Viking style 9th century cross, the shaft of which depicts a serpent biting its tail. In 1891 the church underwent extensive restoration and some interesting Saxon relics were uncovered. In the 10th century Ramsbury was one of the seats of the Wiltshire bishopric, but in 1075 the see was moved to Old Sarum. In 1974 the bishopric was revived and there is now once more a Bishop of Ramsbury. The church contains a very old organ and the family tombs of the Darrells of Littlecote and the Burdetts of Ramsbury Manor, though without their brasses which were stolen or vandalized many years ago. There is a modern plaque dedicated to American servicemen, many of them fliers who were stationed in and around Ramsbury during the war. Some married Ramsbury girls and they made many friends and last year which was the 40th anniversary of D–Day and this year which is the anniversary of victory have brought some of them back to the village in a spirit of wartime nostalgia.

A knot of people had gathered in the main street at the church gate and shortly after our arrival they moved through the churchyard with its grassy mounds and venerable tombstones to the church door, set in a deep embrasured porch and flanked by two beautiful golden leaved trees. Though by no means full the huge chancel held a goodly crowd, sitting stiffly erect in the hard straight-backed pews. It was very dank and cold, for the late afternoon warmth had not penetrated into the interior, but somehow the chill seemed in keeping with the medieval asceticism of the church and the atmosphere inside seemed a curious mixture of austerity and intimacy. The congregation looked typical of any English village, the men ruddy and red-faced from their labours in the fields seeming a little uncomfortable in their Sunday suits and ties. The women, the majority of them middle-aged and motherly, were mostly dressed in well-cut suits and wore the hats beloved by English ladies. Though they were the ordinary folk of a Wiltshire village, they gave an impression of solidity and modest prosperity, of belief in themselves and their country, their pride representative, perhaps of the facets in the national character which defied Hitler and helped achieve the victory being celebrated today forty years later.

The service followed the usual liturgical progression of hymns, Scripture readings, prayers and hymns, with members from the community and the congregation reading from the Bible and leading in prayer. The hymn tunes played on the reedy tones of the old organ were familiar but the words were different, updated and I suppose, more meaningful in the context of today, but nevertheless disappointing to me. I would have liked to have sung the familiar words of my childhood in such a lovely old church. The sermon was preached by a Methodist minister, an elderly man who had been a padre in the war and his discourse was liberally sprinkled with references to his service days. The service was led by a surpliced priest of the Church of England, for this was an ecumenical act of worship designed for people of all faiths and denominations.

Some left the church with tears in their eyes as we stopped at the cross in the churchyard which is Ramsbury's memorial to her war dead. There was a short but impressive wreath laying ceremony and we studied the names engraved on the cross as we had done that morning in Marlborough. I wondered where these Wiltshire lads lie – some in the cemeteries of Northern France and some further afield in Singapore or Thailand. But I felt that many are still remembered not as soldiers or sailors, but as the boys of their home places, known and loved as the individuals they were. And then the time for memory was over and we were back in 1985. We crossed the road to the British Legion Hall where food and drink and good fellowship awaited us. The food, sandwiches, sausage rolls and bread and cheese prepared by the ladies of the Legion, was very good. Simple and wholesome it was typical of village occasions. There were raffles and competitions and drinks were sold at 1945 prices. But the joy and merriment was overlaid with a persistent sadness that would not entirely go away and the talk was mostly of the war. Though I talked to many people, I met none I had known in the old days. Ramsbury had always sent a large contingent to Marlborough Grammar School. They used to travel thither in an old ramshackle bus and I recalled names such as Rosier, Lawrence, Aldous and Ludlow, but saw none who knew them or remembered me.

On the way back to Marlborough we stopped at the small thatched pub in Mildenhall. The landlords are a couple named Cook. Mrs Cook was born in the pub and has lived there all her life. Her husband was brought up in a cottage in George Lane, very close to where we lived. He was a cousin of Stuart Goldsworthy, a classmate of mine at the Grammar School who was killed in the war. There was a festive air in the small crowded lounge bar – victory was in the air, beer was flowing freely and licensing hours had been extended to mark the occasion. Young and old alike were happy, the old remembering their experiences of war, the young participating vicariously, enjoying the party and hoping war would never come to their generation. Oscar produced and put on his American cap and battle jacket – alas, it was too small, – but it added to the spirit of the evening. And then the company broke into song – the songs of the war years being rendered with great enthusiasm if little respect for musicality.

Looking back later that night on all that had happened during the day, I reflected that it was likely to be one of the last such victory celebrations. There will be few of us left in another ten years to remember, rejoice or repine. Surely World War II will be the last global war. Dropping the atom bomb without a doubt brought that conflict to a speedy conclusion, but it gave us a foretaste of the horror of nuclear war. Another such war could well mean total annihilation, no honour, no glory, no bravery, and no victory.

V

HOME THOUGHTS FROM ABROAD

"What does he know of England
Who only England knows?"
Rudyard Kipling

It has been quite challenging for me, living for the last forty years in the United States, to tell this story of Marlborough without recourse to local reference material and the opportunity to interview town residents in depth. Perforce I have had to rely on the slender resources of my own personal library and by going back some 60 odd years in memory. Since completing the main part of the narrative many more thoughts of the past have surfaced – for memories do indeed beget memories – and rather belatedly additional information has come my way which I think should be included at this point even at the risk of it appearing to be out of context.

Dr Dick Maurice has been kind enough to provide me with a good deal of information about his family which has been consistently and continually identified with Marlborough in the field of medicine and civic and cultural service for the last two centuries. I believe it will be of interest to many Marlborough citizens.

It was in 1792 that the first Maurice – Thelwall – began the practice of medicine in Marlborough, coming there from his ancestral home in Lloran Ucha in Denbighshire. Thirteen of his descendants adopted medicine as a career while many of the others served with distinction in other professions and the armed services. Of the thirteen who

117

became doctors, nine became partners in the family practice and today the sixth generation provide two of the town's present doctors. The Maurice's justly claim to be the oldest group practice in the country.

After qualifying as a surgeon, Thelwall's son David joined his father in Marlborough and built Lloran House, named for their Welsh home, on the lower side of the High Street. When I was young it was the residence of Dr Walter Maurice and sometimes church fetes were held in its beautiful grounds. The present-day surgery is an extension of the house, though the dwelling itself is no longer in the possession of the family. David's two sons trained as doctors at St Mary's Hospital, Paddington which was built close to the London terminus of the Great Western Railway. Medical training at this hospital became a family tradition. When the younger son James came to Marlborough he took over and considerably enlarged Lloran House while his father built Manton Grange a large house to the west of the town beyond the college. In 1866 Savernake Hospital was founded with a medical staff of four, two of whom were Maurices. Dr James had a very large family and four of his ten sons took up medicine as a career. Of these four, two practiced in the town, Oliver who died in 1912 and Walter who came to Marlborough after serving eight years in the navy as a surgeon. It was Dr Walter who attended our family when I was growing up. Dr James's youngest son Godfrey became a doctor. Immediately after qualifying he came to Marlborough for a brief period towards the end of the war when there was a severe shortage of doctors. He must have attended our family – we had arrived from Devizes in January of 1918 – for my mother spoke most highly of him. I was of course, too young to remember him. Dr Dick told me Godfrey gave up the idea of general practice after an unfortunate experience trying to deliver a baby in a cottage on Clench Common. Instead he joined the Sudan Medical Service where he had a very successful career, becoming Principal Medical Officer in Khartoum, and engaging in research on the tsetse fly and the sleeping sickness it causes. In the next generation I remember Dr Jim, nephew of Walter and himself the son of an army doctor and Dr Tim older son of Walter and brother to Dr Dick. Each of these has a son serving in the town today.

Mrs Cicely Maurice, first lady mayor of Marlborough in 1954 was the widow of Thomas Maurice who was in the Royal Navy and was blown up with all the crew of a warship in the early days of World War I. Two of Dr James's sons Thomas and Oliver married Miss Giffards, sisters who lived with their parents at Lockeridge House. A nephew of these ladies, Sydney Giffard is at present Britain's ambassador to Japan. The Giffards are a very old family the first of whom came over with William the Conqueror. The Maurices trace their descent back to the 16th century.

Writing so much about the doctors of the town leads me to think of dentists. At the time I was growing up the only fully qualified dentists in the town were two partners named Sayce and Churchill and they practiced in Kingsbury Street. My mother had great confidence in Mr Sayce, a tall thin bespectacled man. Using gas he extracted all her teeth while she was still comparatively young and supplied her with false teeth which fitted well and looked nice. She was very sad when he died suddenly in early middle age. Mr Sayce was a very keen amateur photographer and he once gave my mother one of his photographs which she prized highly. When I left for America she gave it to me. It shows a view from Martinsell overlooking the Pewsey Vale. It hangs in a collection of Wiltshire pictures in my home today, a collection which includes several of Christopher Hughes's etchings and two of my father's marquetry pictures of Stonehenge and Devil's Den.

During my years in America I have often been surprised at the links between Wiltshire and my life in this country which have come to light sometimes in an unexpected fashion. Especially since the publication of *Recollections of a G.I. Bride* I have had many letters from people who have ties with Wiltshire and the Marlborough area. Many are of course G.I. brides themselves. I heard from Monica Siney, now living in Baltimore whose father kept a butcher's shop in Pewsey, from a girl, Mollie Ogilvie, from Urchfont who knew relatives of mine and through whom I was able to trace cousins whose whereabouts I did not know. A copy of the book was purchased in great excitement in a shop in Chapel Hill by a young man who had been born in the Five Alls in London Road. And one Sunday last November listening to the sermon in the University Presbyterian Church in Chapel Hill I heard our erudite and eloquent young minister Dr David Hoffelt quote Richard Jefferies.

'It is eternity now. I am in the midst of it. It is about me in the sunshine; I am in it, as the butterfly in the light-laden air. Nothing has come; it is now. Now is eternity. Now is the immortal life.'

Since Chapel Hill is a university town, it is possible that a few besides myself in the congregation might have heard of Richard Jefferies, but I suspect that only I would know that it was of Wiltshire he was thinking when he wrote of the butterfly in the light-laden air, conveying the very essence of the downs to one who loved but left them.

It sometimes surprises me that I can write so long and – or so it seems to me – so lovingly of a town where I spent only the first eighteen years of my life. Though I am a rightful Moonraker, I cannot claim any deep roots in Marlborough for I was born in Devizes, being brought to Marlborough as an infant of five months. My father by birth and breeding was a Wiltshireman through and through, but living as a child and young man in the village of Alton Barnes, his town connections were all with Devizes rather than Marlborough. My mother, born to parents from Norfolk and Shropshire and herself a native of Herefordshire, did not come to Wiltshire till she was twelve, living then in the villages of Great Cheverell, Erlestoke and Worton, so that her "town" was likewise Devizes. I doubt that Mother had ever been to Marlborough, perhaps never even heard of it, until my father obtained work there in January of 1918. My parents arrived there on a bitterly cold day, at a time when the conduct of the war against Germany had reached its lowest point, to live in a small row house with their two small daughters. They were to spend the rest of their lives there.

Though money was always scarce, we, as a family, lived happy lives in Marlborough, my mother creating a warm and loving home, and my father painting a romantic, yet accurate, picture of the town he grew to know and love, so that I felt from my earliest years that Marlborough was indeed a very special place in which to live. The education that I received at St. Mary's Girls' School and the Grammar School at the hands of fine dedicated teachers expanded my knowledge of the town's history and geography and gradually its whole story began to take shape in my mind.

I left Marlborough in 1936 with very mixed feelings, first to go to Whitelands College in London, then to teach in Birmingham and other parts of the country. At the age of 19 I was anxious to sample life elsewhere and my parents encouraged me to do so. But I endured considerable homesickness for the safe familiarity of Marlborough, especially when the war disrupted our daily lives and brought many complications to my job as a teacher. My periodic visits back to Marlborough were like oases in the desert. By 1944 I had lived in two large cities, several villages and a market town considerably larger than Marlborough. By comparison I decided that so far I had not found a better place than the town I grew up in. It seemed right and proper that I should meet and marry my American husband in

Marlborough and spend a few months with my mother and father before beginning a new life in a new land.

Just as 1985 marked the 40th anniversary of Victory, so 1986 is a special year for the thousands of foreign women, the majority of them from the British Isles, who arrived in the United States or Canada 40 years ago to join the men they married during the war. September 1986 saw a reunion of many of the "brides" in Southampton which was the port of embarkation and last glimpse of England for many of us. What has been the lot of the war brides on this side of the Atlantic? A book recently published in the United States, *Bittersweet Decision* by Helene R. Lee tells of the many and varied experiences of a large number of the women who provided the author with information via questionnaires and personal interviews. Their stories range from grave disillusionment to enthusiastic embracement of their new country. Some returned forthwith to their homeland. Many for a variety of reasons, pride, lack of money, concerns for children, could not or would not go home, so that they learned to accept, adapt and shape their lives accordingly. Whatever the circumstances and ultimate denouement of each individual story, memories of English life and family and friends left behind saddened yet sustained us all.

I was among the more fortunate. Married at 26, I was older and more mature than most who were wed at 18 or 19. I had had somewhat more education too and several years of experience in a career easily transferable from one country to the other should I choose or find it necessary to work. I was fortunate too in where we lived, mostly in the New York area and always in the eastern part of the country which bears the greatest resemblance to England in climate, and way of life. Most important of all was my husband's support and understanding and his family's acceptance of me. Another consideration was his steady advancement in the business world. My mother's death only a few weeks after my arrival in the States severed my strongest family tie with England and my longing for homeland became impersonal – perhaps idealized – but largely a matter for quiet thoughts, kept to myself until I began to articulate them by committing them to paper. Many of the girls found comfort and companionship through the G.I. Bride organizations and the Daughters of the British Empire. The lucky ones went home often and received visits from parents, relatives and friends. With few exceptions all kept a core within themselves that was English and all tried to inject some of their country's customs, ideas and beliefs into the raising of their children.

America has now been my home for over 40 years and it will be so for the rest of my life. The places I have lived in over here, ranging from New York City to the small university town of Chapel Hill in North Carolina are vastly different from Marlborough and the way of life is different too. Suffice it to say that growing up in Marlborough prepared me well for life here, and that living happily here has deepened my love for and understanding of Marlborough. I look back with pride and occasionally with some regret still, but with a degree of knowledge about the town which has been deepened and widened by much thought, considerable reading and memories of childhood sharpened now by advancing years.

I have been fortunate, not only in where I grew up, but also when. The twenties and the thirties, the years between the wars and those of World War II were special times, hard and difficult and sometimes deprived, but full of change and challenge, option and opportunity. Time and place have combined in my life to form a rich reservoir for memory and reminiscence.